# DEATH
BY
# PAD THAI
AND OTHER
UNFORGETTABLE MEALS

# DEATH
BY
# PAD THAI

AND OTHER
UNFORGETTABLE MEALS

*Edited and with an Introduction by* **DOUGLAS BAUER**

 Three Rivers Press • New York

Published in the United States by Three Rivers Press, an imprint of the Crown Publishing Group, a division of Random House, Inc., New York.

www.crownpublishing.com

Three Rivers Press and the Tugboat design are registered trademarks of Random House, Inc.

Grateful acknowledgment is made to Alfred A. Knopf for permission to reprint an excerpt from *French Lessons*, by Peter Mayle. Copyright © 2001 by Escargot Productions Ltd. Reprinted by permission of Alfred A. Knopf, a division of Random House, Inc.

Library of Congress Cataloging-in-Publication Data

Death by pad thai : and other unforgettable meals / edited and with an introduction by Douglas Bauer.
          p. cm.
     Includes bibliographical references and index.
  1. Gastronomy. 2. Food habits. I. Bauer, Douglas.
     TX633.D43 2006
     641'.013—dc22                                        2006012887

ISBN-13: 978-0-307-33784-9

ISBN-10: 0-307-33784-7

Printed in the United States of America

DESIGN BY ELINA D. NUDELMAN

10 9 8 7 6 5 4 3 2 1

First Edition

A hot dog tastes best with a baseball game in front of it.

—Unknown

# 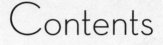Contents

# Introduction

## Douglas Bauer

WHEN THESE TWENTY BOUNTIFULLY GIFTED WRITERS WERE ASKED to search their gustatory pasts for a meal they'd never forgotten and would surely not forget, I explained that I wasn't necessarily interested in the most magnificently prepared, heavenly tasting food they'd ever eaten. I was looking instead for meals made unforgettable by their *occasion*. Occasions that extended the culinary circumference beyond how things tasted to include the more complex palates of love and loss, of welcome and return, of comedy and error, and on and on. For what makes the subject of food the scrumptious stuff of story is not the perfect balance of the recipe or the genius of the chef; it's the narrative of what's humanly at stake as we sit down to eat; what thoughts and emotions are stirred, revived, put in play, by the table we're called to, by those who call us to it. And yet I wasn't looking either for various renditions of Proustian epiphany: Bite into a little cake and . . . how many volumes later? As a way of writing about food, that conceit has become a little wearisome and a lot precious in recent years. If anything, the idea was for a kind of Proust in reverse: not taste evoking memory but rather memory evoking taste.

I'm delighted but not surprised to report that I got deliciously more than I asked for. Herein you will find stories featuring food as the central player in a marvelous array of roles. Dipping into the contents, absolutely at random, there's the story of a woman's lifelong desire, from grade school to the very recent present, for the food in someone else's lunch box, on the plate across the table. And one of a young man's Freudian (the writer's word, not mine) aversion to vegetables, and the beautifully simple ritualistic meal it made him miss, due to paternal expectations that he would take over the family wholesale produce company. There's the account of a couple, struggling on the husband's lowly assistant professor's salary, heading to Manhattan to celebrate the acceptance of his first novel and learning that a full day of fancy New York dining can leave a person nearly broke and utterly famished. As well, there's the hilarious history of one woman's life with lasagna. And the detailing of the planning for a dinner honoring a prestigious poet, encompassing everything from the personalized place cards to the celebratory sestina to, oh, yes, the food. And a blow-by-blow chronicling of the day-long merry massacre of four-pound lobsters in order to achieve pad thai transcendence. There are these and there are fourteen more, each and every one of them delectable. Food as barometer. Food as education. Food as test. Food as reward.

Food as bait. Food as bestowal. Food as magnet. But as varied as the stories are in tone—deeply humorous to wistful to melancholy to antic—the thing that's common among them is the part food plays as offering, as consumable commerce. Food as a gift.

The model, the touchstone, for such forays into autobiography through the taste buds is, of course, the extraordinary work of M.F.K. Fisher. For more than a half century, in more than twenty-five books, she reigned, until she died in 1992, as the supreme chronicler of the human appetite—for food and, implicitly, for other of life's irresistible flavors. Her titles alone say it best. *Serve It Forth. How to Cook a Wolf. The Gastronomical Me. The Art of Eating.*

I said, just above, that she reigned until she died, but as far as I'm concerned she reigns still, and always will. But then I'm biased.

In the early 1970s, when I was twenty-four years old, I spent a week with Mary Frances in New Orleans, that storied and now grievously devastated place, where it was our job, first at lunch and then again at dinner, to eat the city's remarkable food, justly celebrated fare that blends the many seasonings of the region's inimitable history. Briefly, here's how it happened.

I'd been working for a few months at *Playboy* magazine when the executive editor, who had ancestors in New Orleans and loved to eat and loved M.F.K. Fisher's writing, asked her if she'd like to spend some time there in order to describe the city and its food. She said she'd be delighted, but she made one demand. She would need a cohort. If she were to visit any restaurant, an anonymous (as she agreed should be her *modus operandi*) and unaccompanied woman, she'd instantly be steered to the room's Siberia, the dark corner by the kitchen, behind the aspidistra.

I understand, said the editor. And I know just who to send to accompany you. A very bright young woman, the new star of our staff.

No, Mary Frances said. Two women would suffer an identical fate. The dark corner. The aspidistra. The crashing cymbal-sounds of pots and pans every time the kitchen door swung open. No, the cohort must be a man. "I don't care what sex he is," she said, "as long as he wears pants."

I wore pants, and fairly expertly, if I do say so. Otherwise, I cannot fathom why the editor chose me to go. This is not false modesty speaking. I'd never heard of M.F.K. Fisher, had not read a word of her writing. My wife and I had very recently moved from Des Moines to Chicago for my job at the magazine, and in the matter of fine food my idea of an accompanying sauce was mustard or ketchup or a viscous glop of Kraft Miracle Whip, mayonnaise being a bit too subtle and evanescent on my palate.

The fact of my youthful ignorance is mostly relevant to this whole glorious episode because of what it says about the way Mary Frances extended herself to me. Imagining, and over the years I often have, this culturally sophisticated and worldly wise woman—someone who'd spent much of her life in France and Switzerland; had lived among the world's best vineyards, both there and, when I met her, in northern California—coming down from her hotel room to the lobby and greeting the polite young rube who would be sitting across the table from her for a week, it seems to me her first thought might have been that, with any luck, they would seat us behind the aspidistra. But she offered me a warm smile and spoke enthusiastically, in her surprisingly small, melodiously high voice, of the great adventure we were about to commence.

She was a tall woman, then in her early sixties, and somewhat stout. But she was nevertheless beautiful, as she had been and would be all her life. Photos of her through the decades record an early innocent movie-star glamour, truly, and a late, wise and yet more delicate loveliness. What of course did not change as she aged were her high cheekbones and the wide, bright eyes that had the patient penetrating gaze of someone who wished to look at simply everything and understand what she was looking at.

That first day, after saying our hellos in the hotel lobby, we walked a few blocks through the French Quarter to lunch at the fabled Galatoire's. I remember the restaurant as elegantly Spartan, paradoxical as that might sound. Black and white checkered tile floor. Waiters in black jackets and starched white shirts. Ceiling fans revolving with perfect lassitude, a kind of kinetic demonstration, as if to say, Just to remind you, this is the pace at which our city moves. I see it vividly, though I have no idea if what I see is remotely accurate.

Scanning our menus, we devised an excellent strategy we would hold to through the week. Mary Frances would decide what dishes we should order and what wine we should drink and when the waiter came I would tell him what she'd just told me. Hence, we fell easily into the roles for which we were suited. At Galatoire's, she suggested I order for us the restaurant's signature oysters en brochette and a simply grilled pompano, and that, of course, we must christen and launch our culinary cruise with a bottle of good Champagne. And when I had done all that, I looked around, not an aspidistra in sight, and knew I wasn't in Des Moines anymore.

The days fell naturally into . . . a routine? Can sublimity, replicated daily for a week, be diminishingly termed a routine? If so, here was ours: After mornings on our own, we'd meet in the lobby and head out to lunch. Then we'd separate again and reconvene each night at the hotel bar for a Ramos gin fizz and conversation about what we'd seen that afternoon, before walking, usually, or taxiing, if necessary, to that night's dinner.

About that Ramos gin fizz. (In a chilled cocktail mixer, combine 1½ ounces of gin, 2 tablespoons of cream, ½ ounce of fresh lemon juice, ½ ounce of fresh lime juice, 1 fresh egg white, 1 tablespoon of powdered sugar, and 3 to 4 drops of orange-flower water and shake for at least a minute. Strain into a goblet glass and top with ¼ ounce of chilled club soda.) It was a drink, I don't have to tell you, that I was unfamiliar with, and I can't remember exactly how we settled on it. Maybe we watched the hotel bartender deftly mixing one and I decided, what with the egg white and the cream, it was close enough to food. We'd be shirking our assignment not to taste one. In any case, we came up with the idea, a kind of gustatory side bet, that part of our great New Orleans exploration would be to find the city's best Ramos gin fizz.

And so, for a week, we ate and talked and walked and looked and listened, traveling the length and breadth of the city and its environs. I remember that we talked a lot about what was for both of us a time of moving to new lives. Mine in Chicago. Hers in a magnificently simple two-room house on a nature preserve in the Sonoma Valley, one she called, with characteristically provocative candor, Last House (characteristic and also prophetic, for indeed she would live there her final twenty years). However improbably, we were just immediately comfortable with each other. The wide chasm of knowledge and experience and forty years of age that separated us was bridged, at the *heart* of who we were, by a shared small-town Midwestern temperament (Mary Frances was born in Michigan; her beloved father, Rex, was, like me, an Iowan), one that places a priority when meeting someone new on social courtesy and conscious thoughtfulness. As in her writing, she presented in her conversation shaped and shifting versions of her life, marked with slyly partial allusions to people and places. Over the years, having read most of what she wrote, I've thought it fitting that her favored form of sentence-ending punctuation was the ellipsis. Nevertheless, she was, to my great fortune, the perfect conversational companion, both a marvelous raconteur (partial to outrageous declarations matter-of-factly offered: "I woke up the morning after I'd married Donald Friede and I couldn't remember my name for two days") and a genuinely sympathetic listener.

As to the food we ate that week, here's some of what I recall: That that first meal at Galatoire's turned out to be our best. That Antoine's—sadly for Mary Frances, who'd known it when—was a tourist-trap disaster, its oysters Rockefeller an extremely bad idea, extremely badly executed. That exactly one bite of a Central Grocery's renowned muffuletta sandwich, layered with Italian cold cuts, so offended her taste buds that she got instantly a little ill and had to go back to her room and lie down, rising frequently to brush her teeth in an effort to get rid of the flavor, the curse of

perfect palate, thought I, having polished off my own muffuletta and the rest of hers in the time it took us to walk
back to the hotel. That we tried and tried and tried again to
determine whose raw oysters with ketchup and lemon juice
and Tabasco sauce on saltines were better, Felix's or the
Acme's. And who better to try with than the author of a
book called *Consider the Oyster?*

We decided to consider some one last time, late in the
morning on the day she was leaving. We shared a dozen at
each place, after which we surrendered, calling the competi-
tion a brinily ambrosial tie, then broke it, as I remember, by
giving style points to the insouciant élan of Felix's shuckers.

It was by then getting close to noon, the sun overhead
and strong, the humidity declaring itself, the sidewalk clean-
ers' water all but evaporated from Iberville Street. I was staying another day, in part to revisit some of the places where
we'd eaten, requesting menus and asking about certain ingredients in certain dishes. Mary Frances had insisted I not
take her to the airport, and she was saying we should probably be thinking about finding her a taxi when we noticed a
restaurant across the street—I recollect an Irish name;
O'Malley's; Fitzpatrick's; not one we'd heard of or been directed to try—opening its doors for lunch. There was time,
just enough, for a Ramos gin fizz.

The place was spacious, done to suggest a men's club,
wood paneled, New Orleans Saints football helmets and
other sports memorabilia mounted here and there. Mary
Frances and I were the first customers and the bartender
was still setting up, slicing lemons and limes and sticking
toothpicks in olives, working with efficient assembly-line-
robot motions, which he obligingly interrupted to make our

drinks. By now, I'd become entirely familiar with the mixing procedure. I'd imagined varying degrees of excellence in what I'd tasted over the week explained by subtle differences in the way the egg white was separated, the care with which the drops of orange-flower water were added, the rhythm with which the mixture was shaken. So I watched, alert and not entirely self-mockingly so, as the bartender in the restaurant with the probably-Irish name on Iberville mixed and poured and placed our Ramos gin fizzes before us.

After a slow, assessing sip, Mary Frances announced, "This is it." Sipping too, I was quick to agree. We had found it: the perfect Ramos gin fizz. We drank and smiled, and when we'd finished, we walked happily triumphant back out into the wet heat of the day. I hailed a cab and we strongly hugged and I watched, waving, as the taxi made its way down narrow, crowded Iberville, turned at the intersection, and headed for the airport to take Mary Frances back to northern California.

Now a confession. That valedictory Ramos gin fizz was undoubtedly delicious. But I have no idea, and secretly didn't even as I sat there in the company of Mary Frances and mounted football helmets drinking it, whether it tasted any better than half a dozen others we'd enjoyed through the week. But, be that as it may, there's no question she was right in declaring it the best. It was the best one we drank because it was the last one we drank, discovered by fortuitous accident in a most unlikely setting of testosterone decor, mere minutes before our magical week's time was to expire. What Mary Frances tasted was the vital ingredient none of the other Ramos gin fizzes contained, one she looked for whenever she talked and wrote about food: the ingredient of story.

Of course she was vastly, immeasurably knowledgeable about food purely as food: how to eat, what to eat, what else to eat with what you're eating. And as demonstrated by the muffuletta episode, she had, as I said, the gift—or curse—of perfect palate in the way that the most brilliant musicians have perfect pitch. But more importantly, she also knew, and dramatized compellingly in everything she wrote, that when our minds and our hearts as well as our taste buds are stirred, then food is a story and a story is food.

And so, with her life and her work and that fabulous week much in mind, this was the notion in inviting these wonderful writers to the table. With their twenty separate tastes they've proven the notion right twenty times over. What a banquet! *Bon appétit!*

# DEATH

BY

# PAD THAI

AND OTHER
UNFORGETTABLE MEALS

# Foodums

## Sue Miller

WHEN MY SON WAS IN HIGH SCHOOL, AROUND FOURTEEN OR
fifteen years old, he wouldn't arrive home from school until
early in the evening—after sports practice, after showering
and catching the commuter train from Concord to Cambridge, after walking the ten or so blocks from the train station to our house. His last full meal would have been lunch,
a meal he probably would have expended, calorically speaking, by mid-afternoon. He'd step in the front door, drop his
backpack on the floor, and half-moan, half-yell, "Foodums!"
Sometimes, if the wait for supper was going to be more than
ten minutes or so, tears would actually rise in his eyes, tears
of pain, of sheer ravenous hunger.

In those days I thought of myself not so much as a person
who cooked, but as a person who presented edible fuel, so
many calories—thousands at each meal—to a raging fire. In

fact, watching the fork or spoon lift to my son's mouth over and over, occasionally I would remember the repetitive motion of my father, shoveling coal into the furnace in the basement of the house I grew up in: the door swung open, the heat pulsing out, the fire yellow-white and alive inside. My son—Ben is his name—had always been this way around food: in need. In earlier years, the younger children on our child-friendly block would sometimes gather in our kitchen on Saturday mornings when I made pancakes for Ben's breakfast, to *watch him eat them*, to see if he could top his record this time.

Ben, I should add, was never fat. He burned. He never stopped burning, never stopped moving, until he collapsed at the end of the day.

What did I cook? Carbs. Carbs were the dish du jour, every day. The *specialité de la maison*. Who could afford enough meat, even enough *vegetables*, to satisfy such an appetite, such need? Not me in those days, a single parent working in day care. And if, on some special occasion, we *were* having meat, I'd have to give Ben bread first, lots of bread while he waited for dinner to be cooked. Bread to dull the sharp edge of his hunger, so that he wouldn't consume the whole roast, the whole chicken, all of the stew.

Mostly, though, I served carbs in one form or another. Macaroni and cheese, spaghetti, stir-fried rice with vegetables, grilled cheese sandwiches. I wasn't into culinary subtlety. It was all gone in about ten minutes anyway.

It wasn't that I *couldn't* cook in an interesting way. I entertained often, and on those occasions I enjoyed setting out an elegant meal. Sometimes I made an elegant meal for Ben, too, and he liked that. Chinese dishes, French dishes, Italian dishes, he liked them all just fine. But what he *needed* was foodums. Fast, high-carb, in bulk.

Foodums. It's what, when you're the cook and it's demanded, you have to supply. And boring as such food can be to prepare, especially when you've prepared it over and over and over again, it is what most children like to eat.

I wish I'd been fed that way as a child. Instead I remember, for example, the dreaded *kidney stew*, so overcooked that the vegetables were mush—all vegetables were mush until about 1975, I think—and the kidneys had turned gray and hard as rubber. If you'd thrown them across the room, and how I yearned to! they'd have bounced back. It's not called *offal* for nothing. Or tongue. Boiled beef tongue. A very large tongue, also overcooked, sitting like an embodied obscenity on a very large platter. Tongue, intricately curled, particularly at what would have been the back of the throat, and thrust out at you aggressively. Like the meanest kid in third grade: "Nyah! Nyah!" Like the Rolling Stones logo, without the red lips. But curlier, and gray, not pink. When my father picked up the knife and started to slice it, I think all of us winced. Why did my mother cook this way? Frugality, of course. Offal was cheap, and we were poor. But there was some sense of real effort involved on my mother's part at this stage of her cooking life. This wasn't just foodums for her. No, I think she felt that this was the way a resourceful housewife with no money ought to cook. I think she wanted to make interesting meals out of unlikely and inexpensive ingredients.

This was a mistake. We were happier when my father was away and she gave up. He was away often. He was a scholar, and he could make money, money we badly needed, by lecturing at colleges and universities around the Midwest. When he was gone, we often had supper in the kitchen, and were allowed to read at the table. My mother would more or less dump sandwich fixings into our midst—a loaf of sliced bread, packaged bologna and liverwurst, Miracle Whip, lettuce, sliced tomatoes—and we'd happily help ourselves and then sit silently, chewing and working our way through whatever books we'd chosen for this treat.

The problem was that my mother hated cooking, and cooking hated her. A few years ago, I wrote a memoir about my father's death from Alzheimer's disease, which sparked a number of his old friends and colleagues—wonderfully for me—to write to me about their memories of him. One of them, who'd stayed with my parents for a week or so when I was small, recalled my mother as always reading, as lively, and then added, "though she might not have been the best cook in the world."

Folks, sixty years had passed! What could she have served him? Her tuna casserole? "Spanish" rice? *Kidney stew?*

She couldn't cook. Everything at our house was overdone, if it wasn't underdone. Meat was gray. Chicken bled freely when it was cut into. Cakes were made from packages, pancakes from Bisquick. Vegetables came from cans, or later from blocks of green ice. Salads were iceberg lettuce with bottled dressing. Soup was Campbell's. Really, the only good meal of the week was Sunday dinner, which was invariable, roast beef and roast potatoes, both—yes—overdone, but in this case because both would have gone into the oven just before my parents left the house to walk to church—where we four children were awaiting them, having walked over earlier for Sunday school. When we all came home, full of virtue and ready to return to bodily life, the house always smelled wonderful. Smelled better, in fact, than dinner tasted. But we didn't notice that. We didn't know better.

Monday we were back to the regulars. Stuffed green peppers. Stuffed with what? Who knew? Just some *stuff*. Or tongue. Or sawdusty meatloaf with frozen French fries.

Then things changed.

We lived on a street on the south side of Chicago which was being claimed, in those postwar years, by young families with children, some of the fathers faculty at the University of Chicago, where my father also taught, in the Theological School. At a certain point in the late forties or early fifties we became a critical mass, all these children—three or four to a family—all these young, interesting parents. There was a father who ran a social work agency, another who was a psychologist at the university, one who worked at the Field Museum of Natural History, another one who worked at the Art Institute. The wives—the mothers—were all overqualified for the job. It was a lively group, and it was the fifties, the time of gin and bourbon and rye. Of martinis and cigarettes. For us kids, the block was a continuous long game, particularly when the weather warmed and we could be out on the street as soon as school was over, and could stay out until we were ready for supper. For our parents, it was a movable cocktail party, now at this house, now at that.

Of course, they seemed ancient to me then, but I think of them now with something like envy. Imagine it, a group of young people in their early to mid-thirties, vitally interested in the work they were doing, at a wonderful, radical university, all simply having to step outside, head down the street a few doors, and find each other to talk, to argue, to laugh. To drink. No one had a television yet, the computer didn't exist. When the work day was over—the work day of books and ideas, of history and art—you sought company, other life, and on our street, you found it, easily.

They never had dinner parties. There were too many kids around, and maybe—who knows?—the other mothers disliked cooking as much as mine did. Instead they drank. They gathered informally, drifting across the street or down the block several times a week, and gossiped and joked and smoked and laughed. Sometimes there was a party, an arranged gathering, and then they often played games— elaborate charades, word games, games in which they drew each other. There was one I remember called Personalysis, which involved the group's guessing each other's identity based on their written responses to Rorschach inkblots. But mostly they talked, with a premium put on wit. They talked and laughed.

Whenever I tell people that my father was an ordained minister, that he taught at a theological seminary, that many of the other fathers in my parents' group of friends were theologians, too, they assume that my childhood was puritanical, dour, un-fun. Not so. There are, it turns out, many God jokes, most of which I heard growing up. And beyond that, our parents just loved to party.

Which was fine, until you wanted supper—foodums!— and they were nowhere around. We children would slowly have meandered home from wherever we'd spent the afternoon, impelled by hunger. We would gather, waiting. We were not allowed snacks—there was no such thing as snack food in our house—so there was nothing to stave off the growing bite of hunger. Finally we'd cross some line and decide it was time to go and fetch our parents home.

I was often the emissary, sent to whine about us, about the children they seemed to have forgotten down the block, about our starving state. Or maybe I offered to go. Because I liked being there among them, the grown-ups. I liked the looseness, the wild laughter, the bawdy jokes, even when I didn't understand them. And you could actually get some food if you weren't too piggy, too conspicuous about it. Cocktail food. What passed then for cocktail food. Those round, orange Ritz crackers with an equally orangey cheese that was served in a plastic container. Triscuits with cream cheese. Tasteless green olives stuffed with pimiento, or woody black ones, pitted.

But my mother was hard to budge, and usually at some point, maybe on my second or third trip to the Grants' house, or the Winters' or the Cliffs', she would send me home with cooking instructions. Cooking instructions which inevitably began with the same two or three steps. One: put a pot of water on to boil. Two: preheat the oven. Three: take—variably—peas, corn, hot dogs, hot dog rolls, soup, tuna, French fries, chicken pot pies, out of the freezer or the cupboard and put them/it either in the water or in the oven. My parents were usually home, trailing clouds of nicotine, boisterous and boozy, in time for my mother to do the final assembling of the meal. And so I learned to cook, to cook in a certain fifties way. And inevitably, because I liked cooking more than my mother did, I began to elaborate the meals I was sent home to make. Nothing very inventive. If I was to assemble, let's say, a tuna casserole out of Campbell's cream of mushroom soup, noodles, and the essential can of tuna, I might add some chopped celery to supply a different texture, a crunchiness and freshness.

In the summers we went to Maine for a full two months, and there my grandmother presided over meals for the entire assembled family, often twenty people or more. She liked to cook, and once I showed an interest in it, she was glad to have me as her student, her assistant, in the kitchen. Over those summers I learned how to make the dishes she was known for in the family. For the most part nothing fancy: potato salad, deviled eggs, soups. Pancakes from scratch. Gingerbread ditto. A kind of muffin her mother made for her father and named after him: Will's cakes. Yes, there was her signature jellied shrimp salad, and that *was* fancy in a certain preposterous, molded way; but mostly I learned the basics. How to boil eggs and drop them in cold water so they'd be easy to peel. How to peel them, rolling them in the black soapstone sink until their shells crackled. I learned the difference between the hard ball stage and the soft ball stage when making fudge or boiled frosting. I learned that you could cook fresh vegetables, that they didn't have to be prepared for you in a can or a frozen box to be edible. I learned that a salad could be made from grapefruit and red onion slices and avocado. I learned what an avocado was.

And back in Chicago I began to notice food at other people's houses, in other situations. Once I went to the bat mitzvah celebration of a friend at a fancy restaurant and watched the tuxedoed waiter assemble a Caesar salad on a rolling cart pulled up to our table. Some very dark green lettuce, the likes of which I'd never seen, fresh-squeezed lemon juice, anchovies, garlic chopped up into tiny pieces, grated Parmesan cheese, oil, and a raw egg. I'd never tasted anything so wonderful. After various experiments, I was able to duplicate it at home. That was the good news. The bad news was that ever after that, I was in charge of salads. "And would you make us a salad, Susan," my mother would say. "As only you can?" Gradually that phrase got attached, too, to the other simple dishes I'd taught myself to produce. Lasagna. Mashed potatoes. Meatloaf. Beef Stroganoff. Cookies.

I don't mean to suggest that anything like the full burden of cooking in our house fell on me, because that wasn't the case. Like Ben years later, I dragged home from high school late in the day, and I had hours of homework each night. My mother was the cook. It's just that two or three times a week, and almost always on special occasions, I would be asked to prepare something, clearly something she'd been thinking about, she'd been anticipating eating. *Foodums*, my mother was saying to me. I want. I want.

I felt coerced. But what could I do? I liked to cook, and I liked to eat what I cooked better than I liked to eat what my mother cooked. So I cooked. It became routine. Often on college vacations, I'd do most of the dinners when I was home, and I was usually in charge of holiday meals.

I married for the first time young, at twenty, just out of college. My husband was in medical school and I was in graduate school, so we ate oddly. He would arrive home at some preposterous hour, wondering what there was to eat, and I'd throw something together. Later, I worked as a cocktail waitress, and I'd bring him a sandwich from the restaurant kitchen, which he'd eat at one or so in the morning if he'd waited up for me, or take with him for lunch the next day if he hadn't. It wasn't until my son was born a few years later that my life of supplying foodums began in earnest.

M.F.K. Fisher has famously written of our hunger as never being only about food. We wish, in some deeper sense, to be fed. And I think we wish our feeding of others to be received in some parallel deeper sense—as a gift, as an offering of some part of ourselves. Perhaps, playing with the word my son invented, I can speak of several kinds of deeply needed food, several ways of thinking about the food we prepare. There's foodums, yes, and there's also Foodums. Various things in my own history of being fed, of feeding others, have complicated all of this for me. I think it may be in response to a sense of obligation around cooking, a sense of duty, that I'm often a bit slapdash as a cook. In an otherwise lovingly cooked, carefully thought-out meal, there will be something missing—something wrong, something I forgot or screwed up, as though I'm trying to say, "I don't *have* to do this, you know." Pouring the water off the vegetables, I lose my grip and half of them fall into the sink and down the disposal. Oops! No peas tonight. Or I'll assume the presence in my pantry of the critical ingredient for some dish to be prepared at the last minute, and lo! it isn't there. No dessert, guys. Sorry. Once I mistook green peppercorns for capers and set them out with the smoked salmon. Once I served a butterscotchy *soup* that was supposed to have been a caramel pot de crème.

I remember a lively dinner party I threw perhaps twenty years ago for a group of friends—two women writers, the musicologist friend of one of them, a poet I was going out with, and a man new to town who'd been given my name by

a mutual acquaintance and whom I'd invited along when he
called. We had drinks and hors d'oeuvres, we sat at the table
and had a salad, and then I brought out the main course—
a pork stew with apricots, black beans, and . . . uh-oh! no rice.

Where was this missing rice? I'd measured the water into
a pot, I'd set the raw rice out on the counter next to the
stove. But because I was talking and laughing and would
have had to retire to the kitchen at a certain point to add it
to the water, to put it on to boil, there was no rice. No rice
to sop up the juices of those very juicy other dishes. I apolo-
gized, as I always do. I went around the table, pretending to
serve them all the rice I hadn't made: here, here, here, here,
here. And who's to say it wasn't just as good, if a lot messier,
without the rice? Who's to say it wasn't perhaps more gratifying for the guests that the meal wasn't perfect, that the
hostess was a bit of a ditz? Later, we danced, a sign, as I took
it, that all was forgiven, that the evening was a success.

It was four or five months after this that I began to go out
with the extra man at the table, the man new to town whom
I'd included in my almost-gracious dinner party. It was all a
bit tentative and slow. I had just ended my involvement
with the poet, and he'd just broken up with someone else.
On our third or fourth date, he asked me over to his place.
For dinner.

He lived in an old bow-front brick townhouse, in an apartment on the parlor floor, with high ceilings and walls he'd
painted a light gray when he moved in. Next to the Victo-
rian marble mantelpiece, he had angled a red velvet couch.
We sat on this couch as we drank wine; and then we went
into the little galley kitchen, where I boosted myself up on
the counter so he could do this and that with the food. Before

we moved to the table, he put pears in wine, with cloves and a cinnamon stick, and set them to poach in the oven. What I remember about the meal was that smell, the smell of the wine, of the sweet spices, of the pears, intensifying around us.

Though I remember too that the table was small, set up behind the couch at the back of the parlor. That he had china and glasses and silverware and napkins. That he served chicken with a cream and cognac sauce. That it was delicious. That I felt as though I were being given a gift, a gift I hadn't known I needed, a gift made with loving care for exactly the person I was. That I was somehow, suddenly, famished. Foodums! I ate and ate. That we never got to the pears.

Of course, the question is, what are you to do when someone gives you such a gift? I suppose there are many possible answers. Here's mine: Reader, I married him.

## Pears Poached in Seasoned Wine for Two

Approximately half a bottle of full-flavored, inexpensive red wine, such as cabernet franc, merlot, or grenache

1 cinnamon stick

½ cup sugar

2 tablespoons ground cloves

2 tablespoons ground nutmeg

2 firm pears, Anjou or Bartlett, unpeeled and left whole

Pour the wine into a heavy-bottomed pot. Add the cinnamon, sugar, ground cloves, and ground nutmeg and stir. Place the pears in the pot. There should be enough wine so that the pears are approximately half submerged, whether they're standing or floating. Bring the seasoned wine to a simmer. Cover and cook at a low simmer for as long as it takes to eat whatever comes before it, 30 minutes minimum; an hour is fine.

Lift the pears from the pot with a perforated spoon or ladle. Let cool for 2 to 3 minutes. Slice the pears in half, remove the cores, and place in shallow bowls, two halves per bowl. Serve with scoops of the best vanilla ice cream or gelato money can buy. Drizzle a couple of spoonfuls of the wine over the pears and ice cream.

# La Divina Commedia

## Amy Bloom

I AM LOOKING FOR THE PERFECT LASAGNA, MAKING MY WAY through cookbooks at midnight, ready for heartbreak but hopeful, like Dante seeking Beatrice.

I have been making lasagna for thirty years. I am middle-aged and in love and I am counting on lasagna. Marcella Hazan strongly recommends passion, clarity, and sincerity when cooking and she particularly recommends it in the form of *Le Lasagne coi Funghi e Prosciutto*, and I am considering it. Six layers of pasta, béchamel sauce, thinly sliced wild and cultivated mushrooms, prosciutto, and freshly grated Parmesan. I have made it before. It is handsomely reliable. It is a good black dress with pearls. When I read the recipe at half past midnight, I think, No one, not even a man whose mother is a very fine Italian cook, and actually an Italian, could say that you had not made an effort when you take this out of the oven. I wonder if I can bring myself to refer to it as *le lasagne*.

My life with lasagna began when I was cutting classes at Boston University. I wandered across town, into the North End, and discovered real Italian food. Sweet and hot sausage hanging in ropes, *polpette* taken out of a steaming pot and dropped into a paper bucket for me, fresh ricotta in a tub, *bocconcini* of fresh mozzarella bobbing in a steel drum and Parmesan in giant wheels, and red peppers roasted over a hibachi while I watched. No one thought I should be studying Heidegger instead. No one thought I should turn down a single taste of anything. I stayed so long, a woman offered me a drink and I had my first shot of grappa in a paper cup, at dusk on Salem Street. It seemed that the only right thing was to buy everything I could and layer it between sheets of pasta. I cooked all night. (It would not take all night if you did it. I had one frying pan and one stockpot at the time.) I invited everyone I knew to come for dinner and I told each person to bring a bottle of red wine. I was eighteen years old, I had successfully fed twenty people. I had surpassed my mother. I had fallen in love with the entire country of Italy, and when everyone else had gone home, there was a handsome point guard washing my dishes. It was a culinary and social success of such magnitude that I thought, There is no reason to ever make anything else.

I finished college, still making the *tutti con tutti* lasagna. My new husband said he had never eaten anything like it. He was from Minnesota and he meant it. The new husband came with a new stepson, on whom I could practice being a mother, and after I taught him to avoid plaids and stripes, I showed him how to make chocolate chip cookies and I taught him to make three-cheese lasagna. I thought this would ensure that he could impress girls and never go hungry. Lasagna does not let him down and for the next twenty years, he impresses girls so much that if he were not such a decent man, he could choose never to cook for himself at all.

I had my first little girl and when I was trying to work things out with the mothers in her play group, I made Dieter's Lasagna. It had ground turkey breast, whole-wheat noodles, part-skim mozzarella, and fat-free ricotta. One of the other mothers said, "I feel better about myself when I eat this way, don't you?" I did not. I felt that I had betrayed all of Italy. We left the lasagna and the educationally stimulating toys and I drove my daughter all the way to Pepe's Pizza in New Haven. We finished off a small pie and when we got home I washed the tomato sauce out of her hair, which I had expected, but also out of her underwear, which I think must be the sign that you have really, really enjoyed your lunch.

Tempus fugit, and I had three kids and made the World's Fastest Lasagna about once a week. I bought my pesto sauce. I bought my tomato sauce. I bought no-boil noodles (and there was nothing wrong with them at all) and I grated Fontina cheese on every layer. I tossed chunks of Fontina to my children while the WFL baked and they clapped like seals and we agreed that there was nothing wrong with any food that could be caught on the first bounce.

My husband liked to entertain. When I met him, he ate bulgur wheat and lentil casseroles and drank wine out of bottles shaped like fish. Now we'd come to have a whole shelf of Julia Child and Jacques Pépin and eight hundred traditionally shaped bottles in the cellar. I knew more about great wine than I needed to or can now afford to and to this day, I feel an odd, proprietary satisfaction when I see bottles that used to sit on our basement floor going for four hundred dollars apiece. (It's two a.m. and I am thinking of a Barolo we once had. I wonder if it would be too powerful for the lasagna I'm contemplating. I wonder if I can call my former husband at two a.m. and ask if he still has some of that spectacular Barolo and whether it's held up and if he does and it has, would he mind if I came by for a bottle this afternoon. I can almost persuade myself that this would be okay. I've done him some favors, over the years. He might be glad to do me a little favor, I think. He might be charmed by my spontaneity. I have to put the phone in my study, shut the door to my study, put an armchair in front of the door, and then walk to the other side of the house.)

Sometimes my husband and I used to cook together, but not often. Often, I'd make one dish the day before and watch the kids while he cooked. He was a more careful cook than I was or am, and it seemed that there is no way to argue the benefits of careless cooking, if there are any. The virtues of insouciance versus economy of motion. Exuberance versus an evenly browned crust. He used to say things like, "There's a better way to cut that tomato," and I would say the kind of things careless cooks do, and then at some point, I just shrugged, and that is why we got divorced.

One night, ten people I didn't know were coming to dinner. We had a toddler, a baby, and a teenage boy with a driver's license. A good Saturday for me would have been a walk and a shower and a stiff drink. Instead, I made an extremely time-consuming, careful, elaborate, and frankly demented dessert "lasagna." It had guava cream and cream cheese whipped up together and layered between mandoline-sliced pineapple that had been sugared and run under the broiler. Instead of tomato sauce, there were finely chopped strawberries between each layer and a great mound of them sliding over the top. The visiting scholars liked it. The most important guest said he had never seen anything like it and he meant it. My husband was very nice about it, which is why although we do divorce, it won't be for a long time and when it does happen, it breaks my heart.

It is three a.m. I am furious with Anna Del Conte and her *Italian Pantry* cookbook. Her *lasagne* are no *lasagne* at all; they are *reginette imbottite*, literally stuffed little queens, which seems about right for such a fussy and somehow unyielding recipe. You fill a shallow oven dish with a bunch of the reginette, which you have made by cutting your lasagna noodles into half-inch ribbons, each strip with a ruffled edge and a plain one. You can see instantly that you cannot use store-bought lasagna noodles, no matter how high their quality, because you will have to save most of every noodle for something else. Maybe for *regular*-people lasagna, is what I think. The reginette are nicely, predictably filled with ham, spinach, and ricotta; covered with a cheese sauce, and baked some more. It sounds fine for a ladies' luncheon and certainly more promising than the other thing Del Conte has tried to pass off as lasagna: a *timballo de pesce*, which she describes as well suited for the cook "who likes to try any-thing a bit more enterprising." That's her tone. *"Povera,"* I hear her saying. "His mother is Italian. What did he say. 'The best cook in the world?' *Dio mio*. And didn't I hear that his wife, that is his former wife—are they quite divorced?—

was a wonderful cook? I am sure I heard that." (She's from Milan, but her voice in my head is a Maggie Smith drawl, a blend of pity, disbelief, and condescension that makes me want to put my hand through a window.) You see what I'm talking about. I put *The Italian Pantry* behind *Hopi Cookery* and *Our Amish Christmas*. I pour a glass of red wine I can afford. I think about the fact that I have never worried about preparing a meal for anyone in my life. When I met my husband, I was a college student and my ability to cook rice and throw a chicken breast near it was good enough. When I met my girlfriend, I had made a lot of family dinners and was ready to retire. She had made none and was ready to take up the whisk, which she did with great determination and the zeal of a convert. She wasn't crazy about entertaining people, but she loved to cook for them. She made the best flank steak in the world, the most beautifully complex salads, a martini that could peel paint. I never cooked anything ambitious for her in all of our years together. The first year my husband and I were married, he made me a very fancy, old-fashioned seven-layer torte. We didn't have a mixer. I think that we didn't even have a whisk, although that seems impossible. He had blisters on both hands. I feel, acutely, that I am doing penance for all those years of blithe indifference to cookbooks, precision, and something else important which I have been ignoring. If my ex-husband were here, he could make sure I didn't screw up the recipe. If my ex-girlfriend were here, she could just make it for me. I can see them both on the couch, chuckling. This is a very good night for my former partners.

At four a.m., I take the big yellow *Gourmet Cookbook* to bed with me, my hand on page 234's Beef and Sausage

Lasagne recipe, which follows the unappealing Mushroom, Radicchio, and Smoked Mozzarella Lasagne and the elegant vegetarian Butternut Squash and Hazelnut Lasagne—which sounds perfect if I am entertaining an elegant vegetarian, which this man is not. I wake up at five a.m. as if someone has stuck a fork in my cerebral cortex. Six Advil and twenty minutes later, I am in the supermarket with the other people who shop at dawn. We are people coming off the night shift in crumpled uniforms and spattered scrubs; a few young mothers with their crumb-covered babies; old people, self-sufficient and unable to sleep. The cashiers are kinder at this time of day; they are like old-fashioned nurses; their brisk, firm manner discourages the weepy fatigue and self-pity people like us are prone to. But, we are not a bad group of shoppers; no one brandishes a fistful of coupons, no one bangs on the butcher's door, demanding exactly four fresh chicken livers, no one screws up on the self-checkout line. We are dogged.

Sleep-deprived and moonstruck, I hear the boxes of no-boil noodles and the twenty-eight-ounce cans of whole tomatoes in juice call to me and they do not say reassuring things. They say, "How old *are* you, anyway?" They say, "Do your children know where you are?" The flat-leaf parsley waves at me with the cheer of the truly malicious and I end up buying two pounds of it because I cannot remember what a quarter cup looks like. I picture Augusto on a recent bad day, dark circles under his eyes, overdue for a haircut, harried and out of sorts. I am so blinded by love, I bang into one of the young mothers and her baby. The baby lifts his sippy cup grandly, up and over me, like Queen Elizabeth christening a ship. I smile at the apple juice running onto my shoulder and she smiles and the young prince smiles and wipes an animal cracker on my sleeve and I have no idea what to do with all the love that is flooding the grocery store.

I pick up and put down the package of ground veal. The veal is not feeling the love. The veal says to me, "You have refused to buy veal on principle for the last twenty years. Look at you. Slut. Collaborator. For shame." The veal is still talking when I get to the little Italian grocery store for the fresh ricotta and the homemade sausage. The old lady wrestling with the giant pan of eggplant Parmesan nods. We have done this a couple of times a year for the last five years. She nods, I nod. Suddenly, this seems terrible to me. And, also, I see what she sees. A woman in faded track pants and a dirty T-shirt, wearing a bright orange hoodie borrowed from someone much younger. My hair is blowing around like a dark and graying cloud and it seems possible that word could get back from this old woman to Augusto's mother and that the word on the Italian Madre circuit will not be that I am a lady in the living room, a genius in the kitchen, and exactly what I should be in the bedroom but that I am a nearsighted and short-tempered writer with so many bad habits, you wouldn't wish me on anyone's son. I am dabbing at my eyes and putting my things on the counter. I seem to have bought enormous purple figs, moaning ripely in their green box, and prosciutto to drape over them, like a silk slip, and a wedge of Gorgonzola, already crumbling moistly in its wax paper and the old lady elbows her son out of the way to ring me up and say, very kindly, Making a nice dinner?

I say, Yes, I am making a nice dinner. I say that I hope it will be nice. I am almost bent over with hoping that it will be nice and that I am not making a small and significant error in judgment today, which will turn out to be just one of a galaxy of errors in judgment, including my two previous marriages and divorces and, in the middle of the galaxy, very large, with a dozen rings around it, is the terrible idea that I might ever try again. The old lady hands me a tissue and rings me up. She says, Lasagna? I say, Yes, lasagna. A very simple one. Veal, beef, and sausage. The veal, she says, you don't got. She calls to her son, who grinds another half pound of veal for me. Little calves are suffering horribly for me and I feel very bad about this but this recipe is the only thing that stands between me and my fears. The old lady rings up the veal and she says to me, You got a nice wine. I say that I have a nice enough wine, and we both shrug. We are both thinking, two bottles would be a good idea. She says, You got a nice dessert? I don't. I had planned to make tiramisù, which I can do in my sleep, but not today. The old lady puts four cannoli in a box. I look dubious, if it is possible to look dubious, lovesick, and terrified all at the same time. He's Italian, she says. You bet, I say darkly. Very. His family? From Canino, I say. She wraps red and white twine around the box. Aha, she says, big sweet tooth.

I cook all afternoon. It is a wonderfully straightforward recipe and even as I am weeping over the onions, I think, I can do this. I set the table. Twice. I shower and try on clothes that seem appropriate for the occasion, although I cannot bear to characterize the occasion. I have nothing to wear. I think, I cannot do this.

He is pleased by everything. He eats everything. We laugh all night. He tells me stories. I tell him stories. He washes the dishes. We finish the wine. We go to bed. We marry and grow old in Italy. We die in each other's arms.

# Fried Peppers
## Michael Gorra

ONCE A YEAR I MAKE A POT OF RATATOUILLE, IN LATE SUMMER
when the farmers' market in my town begins to fill up with
red peppers and everything in the pot except the olive oil
and maybe the garlic is local. And I don't take short cuts. I
salt the eggplant and let it sit in a colander with the water
draining out, and I cook everything separately, four frying
pans on the stove at once, with a Dutch oven waiting for
them all on the counter next to a board of chopped tomatoes. I'm not sure it's any better that way—the final prod-
uct is always a little bit mushy—but I enjoy the ritual, and
the mess.

This year I chopped a mix of red and green peppers and
blistered their skins in hot oil before tossing in some garlic
and turning the burner down. Twenty minutes, thirty, with
a low flame and a bit of salt while I chopped onions and

zucchini. Few vegetables are more transformed by cooking. Crunch a wedge of raw red pepper and you will feel the vitamins pop in your mouth, but heat makes it like candy. I cook peppers a lot, for *pipérade* or pasta, and few things go better with a steak than a tangle of their soft thin slices. Still, I don't have them in the house as a matter of course; they're not like potatoes or garlic, things I buy no matter what I'm cooking. So as I got to work this Labor Day morning I was conscious of them, of the lobes in my hand and the cluster of seeds at the stem and of my knife at work slicing.

Oh, I'm sick of it, we all are, of this business of food and memory. I don't ever want to read again about what somebody's grandmother cooked, and sometimes I wish I'd never heard of Proust. So much from a little cookie, A. J. Liebling once wrote, and wondered what the Frenchman could have done if he'd only had Liebling's own appetite, and had set his memory loose on "a dozen Gardiner's Island oysters, a bowl of clam chowder . . . [and] a thin swordfish steak of generous area." I read those words for the first time in a foam-filled bathtub at the Château Frontenac, and rereading them now floods my brain with a whole string of years I'd rather not think about. Better mind the peppers instead. They cooked away, and their edges caramelized, the smell filling the house and drifting out the window. The pan sizzled and the peppers cooked and I inhaled as deeply as I could, and then suddenly I knew that Proust was right and that nothing I might do could save me as the kitchen around me fell away and was replaced by a chipped yellow ceramic bowl, covered with a tea towel and sitting on top of three stacked cases of iceberg lettuce.

My father ran a wholesale produce business in Connecticut, and as a boy I spent summers and Saturdays working for him, wheeling hand trucks loaded with sacks of potatoes, unloading trailers full of watermelons, weighing, counting, talking, swearing. It was a family business; it had been his father's and he hoped it would be mine. In the summer the work came fast and long and hard, because we lived on the coast, with beaches and tourists. Then it would fade out over the fall, until after Christmas we'd spend a few months in the red, with the hours short and the help cut back to a small full-time crew, before it would grow again in the spring and we'd start to make money once more. Memorial Day was the signal for something like three months of final exams. Winter felt as slow as a college out of term, and on Saturdays some of the help would stay on after the work was done, playing cards and drinking Michelob. But first came the peppers.

Around eleven a.m. in February or March a short, slight man named Nate would fill a sack with the best peppers we had on the shop floor, and then head out the door for home. Nate only worked for us on Saturdays. His real job was with the city, as a watchman out at the reservoir; a job solitary and dull, but responsible. He had a kind, lean face and glasses that made him look like a teacher, and he always wore a workman's uniform: matching pants and shirt in gray or khaki, the kind gas station attendants wore then, only without the pocket patch that announced your name. His own name was a ridiculous one, at least if you put it into English: Nate not for Nathan but Natale, the Italian for Christmas. And his last name was Boccalini, or little pot, which is the name of a small pottery cup, a footless hand-size bowl from which you gulp house wine. I guess it's no sillier than being named Carter or Short, and Googling it now I find it once belonged to a Renaissance satirist from Perugia.

Which makes sense, Perugia. Nate was in his early sixties, but though he was of the same generation as the other old Italians who worked for my father, he seemed also somehow different. Perhaps it was the glasses, but his face in my memory now seems to belong to the north—anyway, not Sicilian. Toward noon he would reappear, with that bowl and its tea towel covering—I remember that because at home we would have used aluminum foil instead—and with three long torpedoes of crusty, sponge-centered bread tucked under his arm. We'd finish things up—loading a truck, sweeping broken cabbage leaves off the floor—and after a few minutes people would begin to gather around the stack of lettuce where Nate had put his offerings down. Usually it was next to the drinking fountain whose icy water was my father's one concession to luxury. Nate would produce a spoon, the tea towel would be folded back, and a smell of sweet spice would draw us toward him. But to what?

A sword of bread would appear, pulled from its crisp white paper scabbard. Was there a knife? I don't think so; Nate used his thumbs, jamming them into the loaf's end and then scooting them down its length, spreading that bread open, filleting it. And then he'd gather his fingers together and scrape out the insides. It was the best bread in the city but by our standards today it was hardly artisanal—a bit industrial, in fact, with its insides mostly air. In any case Nate wanted a trough, something into which he could ladle the bowl's contents. Tear off a chunk, and scoop. There was a touch of garlic in the air, and olive oil, and I could see the parsley, but the rest of that bowl was a stew of peppers. They were the kind my father called *suntans*, the splotchy green ones that were starting to ripen their way toward red. In the early 1970s that was the best we could do for most of the year. Red peppers were, in effect, seasonal, and those lipsticky Holland hydroponics wouldn't show up for another decade or more.

Scoop and slap a lid on it, wrap it in a paper towel. The outer casing of crust wrapped itself around the soft hot filling, with the juices starting to show through, and Nate handed it off to Charley Muscarella, our oldest employee. Some of the other men were suspicious the first time that bowl appeared, the swamp Yankees and the French Canadians. How could you have a sandwich without meat? Strange. And as for me—well, I gobbled down the bread, but wouldn't touch the peppers. This memorable meal was one I didn't eat.

It was a Freudian thing, I say now, and maybe there's some truth to it. My father sold vegetables and I wouldn't go near them. Salad was all right, because of the crunch and the dressing, and corn, and any kind of potatoes except mashed. I ate almost all sorts of fruit, though for years I had a grudge against the carrot-colored cantaloupe. But not vegetables, and I will put it politely by saying that this was a topic of some debate. No accident, then, that when I *did* start to eat them it was in a form unknown at home. Bamboo shoots, water chestnuts, whatever it was that went into my first mu shu pork—Chinese restaurants made even the familiar unloved onion seem wondrous and strange, and soon enough I crossed over into a stir-fry of Szechwan beef and peppers. Some of these vegetables were strange in themselves, things we didn't sell, and others were cooked in ways I didn't expect, seared and seasoned and mixed together with scallops or chicken, not segregated off into a separate part of the plate. I welcomed that unfamiliarity; and of course my father was not about to eat green beans with ginger and garlic.

Yet the more I think about it the less that vulgar Freudianism seems to explain things. Or maybe it explains the sense of dread with which I approached a vegetable, but not my actual dislike of their home-cooked taste. Because those Chinese chefs knew how to cook vegetables, and neither of my parents did. At home broccoli wasn't blanched but boiled until the kitchen stank, and then dropped, unsalted, onto the plate with a pat of butter. Brussels sprouts the same, green beans, too. I think my mother even boiled summer squash, for how else can I explain its watery yellow chunks? She was Irish, came from a family of not terribly good plain cooks, and hated vegetables herself, having encountered too many childhood wedges of boiled cabbage. She cooked them only because my father liked them. But what explains him?

Both his parents had come from Lebanon as children. He, however, wanted to be unambiguously American and was the only one in his generation of cousins who never learned Arabic. He didn't even like the food, though at church potlucks he would look skeptically at other women's cooking and boast, long after her death, that his mother's cabbage rolls had been tighter and more delicate than anyone else's, her walnut pastries flakier. But I didn't taste hummus until college, and my father ate his vegetables like a Puritan. Or at least at home he did, for now I see him walking across the shop floor to that yellow bowl, and Nate's smiling face, pleased that the boss is hungry; while I take a second piece of bread myself, and linger in that pungent aroma, loving it but not yet daring to do more than smell.

Of course my father wasn't the only person to live on badly cooked vegetables. All this was in the great interregnum, when the immigrants' diet had pretty much died out, and a new cuisine was not even yet struggling to be born. The only herb we sold was parsley: no basil, no cilantro, no thyme. All mushrooms were white, and red leaf lettuce was a novelty nobody was sure would last. Kiwis were exotic, and at that point they all still came from New Zealand. We got turnip and collard greens by special order only, when the soul food diner called for them, but not kale, let alone the *cavolo nero* that has been on every farm stand these last few summers. Mesclun—ha! The business depended on iceberg lettuce and unripened tennis balls of tomatoes, on crates of cabbage for coleslaw and frozen French fries.

Every now and then, as I loaded a truck, I would startle myself with the realization that all this was food, that people would eat it, cook it, and sit around a table and hope to enjoy it. For a bare flicker of a second I would understand, as I shoved a crate of carrots into the corner of a pickup, that this business didn't just give us a living but that our products enabled other people to live, too; that it was sustenance, and deserved an almost sacramental respect. But most of the time the stuff on my hand truck was just a commodity, not quite pork bellies but not all that different either, except that it could spoil and leave us with a lake of rotting lemons. And in this shop full of food, there was surprisingly little to eat. A stick of celery, a banana if you could find a ripe one; most stores wanted them green. Sometimes we'd find a melon with a spot on it—something we might cut around but couldn't sell. Though most fruit was carefully packaged, with each piece precisely placed and counted. You couldn't pull out a plum; it would make a hole and the customer would complain.

Every time I go to the supermarket now I wonder what my father would have made of pluots and daikon radishes, of tomatilloes and the dozen bulbous varieties of winter squash, of blood oranges and frisée. I suspect he'd enjoy the greens I cook for my daughter, searing them in a hot pan with olive oil and garlic, or the slow-cooked parsnips we serve alongside roast pork. He would have had fun with all these colorful new things to sell, and by the time he died, in 1987, he had indeed begun to handle a few of them. I spent the early years of that decade in northern California, and I remember a visit from my parents in the spring of 1982, when after a day in San Francisco we drove over to Berkeley for dinner. It was not, to be frank, one of Chez Panisse's best nights, with the dessert on the fixed menu replaced by an almond tart that was clearly last-minute, as though something had gone wrong in the kitchen. I remember my father grumbling about the inverse ratio of the bill to the portions, and afterward we all had ice cream from a shop down the street, and felt better; though I'm not certain that even if the kitchen had been on we would have been able, yet, to appreciate the simplicity of pure flavors and perfect ingredients. But one thing did make that evening worthwhile. The salad contained something that at first sight we thought was red cabbage. Yet no cabbage has the bitter bracing taste of chicory, and when my father asked about it the waiter went back into the kitchen and came out with a box of radicchio. It was all imported then, and none of us had ever heard of it; but my father was selling it within a week.

What Nate Boccalini had in that bowl was a humbler version of what Berkeley tried to offer us. The peppers were good ones, that I know, the garlic, too, and he had cooked them with care and a practiced hand. Certainly it bore a closer resemblance to actual Italian cooking than anything at our town's checkered tablecloths. The bread was as good as that time and place could provide, and most of the men gathered around Nate's bowl were old enough to remember their mother's immigrant cooking, the simplicity of something near poverty. Would this meal of bread and fried peppers have been so memorable if I'd been willing to eat it? I don't know. But what I would like to know, now, is what else went on in Nate's kitchen.

A few years later we were driving through town together, making a number of small deliveries—a box of tomatoes here, some lettuce there, a sack of potatoes to a diner. It was a dull run, on narrow streets with lots of traffic, and most of the time we had to double park. I was driving by then, a pickup truck with gears that ground no matter how carefully I shifted, and about halfway through Nate asked me stop at a place for which we had nothing that day, an Italian restaurant called the Gondolier. He disappeared inside, and a few minutes later came back out with a box, something he'd had the chef order for him from a supplier in New York.

Inside was an enormous wedge of Parmigiano, fifteen or twenty pounds of it. At home our parmesan cheese came in a paper cylinder from Kraft. "Don't you have to grate it?" I asked, as he took out a pocket knife and cut me a piece the size of a quarter. He shook his head, told me just to let it melt in my mouth. Sharp salt, and sweet, too, with its grains dissolving against my tongue, a taste complex and rich and yet so balanced and overwhelming and new that I can't really break it up into its constituent flavors. It was all one, and I had never, have never, tasted anything else so good. That's my last memory of Nate. I moved away a few years later, and I don't know when he died. Certainly I don't remember seeing him at my father's own funeral. It's only in frying peppers that he has come back to me so forcefully, making me realize just how much he knew about food, and the next time I walk into a *salumeria* and smell that pungent sawdusty aroma in which olives and cured pork and hard cheese all mix, I know I will see his face across the counter.

# Full

## Elizabeth McCracken

I COME FROM FOOD THE WAY SOME PEOPLE COME FROM MONEY. Food was the medium I grew up in, what we talked about, what shaped our days. Jelly omelets, ham steaks, banana splits, tuna noodle casseroles, cupcakes with thick greasy frosting, soft-serve ice cream in flat-bottomed non-cones: we ate to celebrate, we ate out of nostalgia, we ate and ate. If I behaved at the grocery store of my early years, a place called Disco-Mart in the pre-Disco world of Portland, Oregon, my mother would buy me a large sandy cookie from the bakery, where they rubber-stamped my Cookie Club Card: when your card was filled up, you got a free cookie, which delighted me even though I was a child and therefore all cookies I ever ate were free. On really good days, we would stop at the Disco-Mart lunch counter. My brother and I always ordered the hamburger plate, which came in a red plastic basket lined with wax paper, crinkle-cut French fries heaped beside it. The basket and paper were part of how the hamburger and fries actually tasted: it made a difference, that the paper held up the ketchup but did not absorb it; it made a difference that the basket was boat-shaped, punched from a sheet of plastic.

I come from food, and eventually I married into food, which is lucky: the ability to eat anything comes in handy when marrying a person from another country, as I did. (My husband is from England. If you think this is not such a big challenge, gustatorially speaking, you have never been exposed to Marmite.) I am an eater from a long line of eaters, a gourmand instead of a gourmet. Why do gourmets get all the credit? Gourmandism is a kind of social grace, too; we eaters are delightful guests. From an early age I have been comfortable with food in all its denominations, breakfasts (continental, buffet, full English), brunches, lunches, snacks, teas, dinners, banquets. I eat pop-top pudding, Yorkshire pudding, blood pudding. I can put away anything—liverwurst, foie gras, a second dinner—and my hosts will never know it was not precisely what I most wanted in the world. My palate may not be silver, but it is durable, kindly, democratic. It has always served me well.

My grandmother—my mother's mother—always said that my father was a gourmet cook. By this she meant that what he cooked for her on special occasions she admired but could not quite absorb, like experimental opera or abstract art: it was highbrow, certainly, but it sure wasn't brisket. Brisket was comprehensible, and coleslaw and apple crumble and chopped liver, all of her specialties. She pronounced her son-in-law's cooking *beautiful* and ate it dutifully, which hurt his feelings: he'd meant his meals to be delicious above all other things. My mother was the main cook in our house, so delighted by gadgets that she'd make tuna-fish salad in the Cuisinart, but when we moved to Boston my father took over Sunday brunch. This was during the early to mid 1970s, when brunch seemed to be a matter of national importance, like Whipping Inflation Now or lowering the thermostat. Back then, in the years before the invention of cholesterol or at least the discovery of the effects of it on the Mc-Cracken constitution, my father was an enthusiastic, cream-based, ambitious cook. He could turn the kitchen decor from orange and purple—I told you it was the seventies—to béchamel in the process of brewing a preparatory cup of coffee. There was something Shakespearean to the chaos my father the English professor created in the kitchen: the dozens of pots and pans and bowls and whisks seemed not merely dirtied, but vanquished for some noble cause. At six foot three, he could get batter into every corner of the room, and my memory of the kitchen on those Sunday mornings is of a kind of high-fat Carlsbad Cavern, with stalactites and stalagmites of butter, cheese, flour, and cream, the insistent sound of the cats licking the counters, the softer joyous sound of the dogs licking the floor. Out of ceremony and necessity, we ate brunch in the dining room instead of at the kitchen table. My father would cook the same thing for months on end before finding a new enthusiasm. There was the cheese soufflé phase, and then the cheese soufflé with asparagus phase. (I'm the only person I know who doesn't much like hollandaise sauce because I was forced to eat too much of it as a child.) For a while he baked an enormous and delicious brioche every week, and then he became enamored of visiting a fish shop down on Atlantic Avenue in Boston and buying whatever was fresh. "The bluefish is much maligned," he would say, and to me bluefish is still comfort food. This is possibly because my father would cook a bluefish fillet in a stick of butter. Maybe the fish brunches began as a health kick, though I don't remember a single wedge of lemon on the table, just butter and bacon. I can still recall the first time I saw my father getting ready to roast a pan full of bay scallops, each one wrapped in a tiny bacon stole, like pale, plump rich ladies getting ready to go to the theater. I thought he'd invented the concept; I thought he was a genius.

But these are meals made memorable by repetition. Maybe the plenitude is the problem: when I try to remember a single meal, the dishes, the guests, the conversation, I fail. I remember the surroundings but not the company, or the dessert but not the side dishes, or the notable disaster—at one Thanksgiving meal in a restaurant, a harried waitress dropped a family-size bowl of mashed potatoes all over my mother, which turned out to be just enough to cover my mother in a burkha of spuds—but nothing else. I can remember emotions: once at a house of relative strangers, I declined a second helping of soup because I was saving room for the main course, only to realize that I was being offered seconds because the soup *was* the main course. Potato? Carrot? Peanut? The mortification I remember; the ingredients I don't. I remember the feeling of tremendous luck when my husband and I first stumbled upon what ended up as our favorite restaurant in Paris, and even what we ate—wild boar stew with noodles on the side, a glass of the house Côtes du Rhône—but that I remember mostly as a prelude to other meals. (But really, there should be a name for the exalted state of the traveler who discovers a great restaurant without any of the usual gastronomic compasses.) Also in Paris: the night our friend Jonathan (we're pretty sure) was mistaken for a restaurant critic: as the waitress toted up our bill on the paper tablecloth, she informed us comically that we did *not* have a second bottle of wine, we did *not* each order desserts, we did *not* have two Poire Williams apiece, we need not even mention the free chocolate Easter eggs. A non-Catholic, I've never been so absolved of sins in my life, and it was de-lightful, the end of her pencil pointing at my glass, still sticky with eau-de-vie. *You didn't just drink that, you shouldn't have to pay.* I did drink it, as well as its predecessor, which is perhaps why I cannot tell you the full story of that meal.

A memorable meal, surely, should have a plot, not just a punch line. The foreshadowing of the hors d'oeuvre, the deepening of the main course, the suspense of cheese or dessert (depending on what country you're in), the resolu-tion of the dessert or cheese, a little epilogistic brandy. The meals of my life are fond memories, mere paragraphs. There is not a single cheese soufflé that I could pick out of a line-up of cheese soufflés, no jelly omelet that is unlike all other jelly omelets.

But there is at least one pork chop of blessed memory.

I was a child, probably eleven, and home alone sick. Chances are I'd spent the morning watching *Batman* reruns on TV. Both my parents had full-time jobs and generally my mother dealt with kids sent home from school. (My poor mother! She cooked most meals, she took care of us when we were sick, which means, of course, that I can barely remember her doing either.) At any rate on this particular day my father left work to check on me. He'd been to the grocery store. I don't know what I was suffering from—the usual suspects, strep throat or feigned stomachache, would have precluded much eating—but I do know that my father, who only ever cooked extremely fancy food, and only ever on Sunday morning, fixed what was then hands-down my favorite meal: broiled pork chops, crinkle-cut French fries, and the kind of tiny peas in butter sauce that come in a plastic bag you drop in boiling water. He served it in the dining room. We sat at the dark Danish table, my father, as usual, at the head, me, as usual, at his left, and never in my life was I, never in my life will I ever be, more impressed with the care someone has taken to cook me a meal. Daytime, my father at home, not hurrying back to work, the peas and French fries in the same stainless-steel dishes he served asparagus from on Sunday mornings. All this matter-of-fact fuss over me.

I have never forgotten it.

# Home

## Andre Dubus III

MY MOTHER WAS TWENTY-EIGHT YEARS OLD WHEN SHE AND MY
father first separated. She had four kids, all of us under the
age of ten, and we lived in a rented house on a pond in New
Hampshire. I was nine, and so it seemed like a house, but it
was really a summer camp which we rented all year long.
Downstairs was the kitchen and its worn linoleum floor, the
small living room with the black-and-white TV we saw the
Vietnam War on every night; it's where we watched news
about the killing of Martin Luther King; it's where we saw
X-ray photos of Robert Kennedy's brain and the .22 caliber
bullet shot into it; it's where we watched a man walk on the
Moon, my mother sitting on the arm of the couch in shorts
and one of Pop's button-down shirts, saying, "We're on the
Moon, you guys. We're on the fucking *Moon.*"

My father, thirty-one years old then, was earning seven

thousand dollars a year teaching at a junior college over the border in Massachusetts. He'd published his first book, a novel, and was beginning work on the short story. He had a brown beard he kept trimmed, and he was fit and lean from his daily five-mile runs, a ritual he had begun in the Marine Corps a few years earlier. My mother and father rarely had the money to go out to a restaurant, but they hosted a lot of parties at our house, usually on Friday or Saturday nights, sometimes both; my mother would set out saltine crackers and dip, sliced cheese and cucumbers and carrots; they'd open a jug of wine and a bucket of ice and wait for their friends to bring the rest: more wine, beer, bottles of gin and bourbon. Most of their friends came from the college where Dad taught: there was an art professor, a big man who wore black and had a clean-shaven, handsome face and laughed loudly and looked to me like a movie actor; there were bearded poets and bald painters and women who taught pottery or literature or dance. There were students, too, mainly women, all of them beautiful, as I recall, with long shiny hair and straight, white teeth, and they dressed in sleeveless sweaters or turtlenecks and didn't wear bras, their bell-bottoms hugging their thighs and flaring out widely over their suede boots.

The house would be filled with talk and laughter, jazz playing on the record player—a lot of Brubeck, Gerry Mulligan, and Buddy Rich. From my bed upstairs I could smell the pot and cigarette smoke. I could hear the music and the animated voices of my mother and father and their loud, intriguing friends, and as I drifted off in the bed across from my brother, grown-up life seemed to me like some grand carnival and if it weren't for all the dead bodies on TV, I could hardly wait to get there myself.

This was before the real fighting started. My parents must've tried to keep it from us because it seemed to happen only late at night, both of them screaming at each other, swearing, sometimes throwing things—pots or pans, a plate or glass or ashtray, anything close by. They were both raised in southern Louisiana and when they fought, their accents were easier to hear, especially my mother's, "Goddamn you, you sonofa*bitch*." Pop's voice would get chest-deep and he'd yell back at her as if she were a Marine under his command.

Many nights my brother and two sisters and I would listen from the stairs in our pajamas, not because we enjoyed it but because it was easier to bear when we weren't hearing it alone in our beds. But by morning, the sun shone through the trees and most of the thrown or broken dishes in the living room would be picked up, the kitchen smelling like bacon and eggs, grits and toast and coffee, the night before u bad dream already receding back into the shadows where it belonged.

It was the 1960s, and despite what may've looked like a bohemian household with all its parties, books and records, the framed art on the walls, my mother was a full-time housewife, a term we don't use anymore. And while I don't believe she ever liked housework, I know she loved to cook; it was, and is, one of her essential gifts, something she didn't know herself until they were already married nearly a year. They were living on the Marine base in Quantico, Virginia, and she'd cooked her first Thanksgiving dinner for her and

Pop and my older sister, Suzanne, an infant at the time. My mother roasted a turkey she'd stuffed with cornbread dressing. She boiled green peas and baked side dishes of creamed onions and sweet potatoes covered with melted marshmallows. She laid out a bowl of chilled ambrosia—sliced grapefruit and oranges she'd sprinkled with shredded coconut. But it was her gravy that began to convince her she might have a knack; she'd made it from scratch from the turkey's drippings and it came out smooth and dark with just the right amount of game and salt. It was actually as good as her mother's down in Fishville, Louisiana.

We lived in New England, but at supper time our house smelled like any south of Memphis; Mom fried chicken, or simmered smothered steak or pork, all served up with rice and gravy and baking powder biscuits. On the side there'd be collard greens or sliced tomatoes, cucumbers, and onions she'd put ice cubes on to keep crisp. She baked us hot tamale pies, and macaroni and cheese, or vegetable soup she'd cook for hours in a chicken stock then serve in a hollowed-out crust of French bread, its top a steaming layer of melted Cheddar.

This was country cooking, and I remember most of it being those smothered dishes, which she prepared most often because that was the way to make cheap cuts of meat taste rich; she'd take a few scrawny breakfast steaks, season and flour them, then cook them in a beef stock with onions and garlic, steaming the stew out of them, cooking them down to that gravy, that warm, dark, make-you-feel-full gravy.

On our birthdays we could have whatever we wanted for our supper, and she'd cook it. My brother and sisters asked for new dishes every year, anything from grits and smothered steak to pork chops or chicken and sausage gumbo. One year my brother asked for fried frog legs, another year Chinese food, and Mom got hold of a Chinese cookbook and probably went to some specialty shop somewhere for most of the ingredients. She made fried wontons, egg rolls, fried rice, and mu shu pork. Another year she baked Suzanne a cake with hard-candy butterfly wings rising up out of it. She must've been up all night sculpting that, sticking those Necco wafers together with frosting, fashioning them into the shape of wings.

On my birthday, though, I always asked for the same meal, one that never changed: pot roast, rice and gravy, green peas, pear salad, and homemade German chocolate cake.

Each night when Pop came home from teaching, Mom would be cooking in the kitchen and they'd have Cocktail Hour, which meant none of us kids was allowed in there while they sipped Jim Beam and our father unwound and told Mom his day and she told him hers. My older sister constantly had her feelings hurt by this; she wanted to be in that kitchen with them, sharing her day, too. But I didn't feel that way; I could never quite get the echoes of their late-night arguments out of my head; I wanted them to spend as much time together as they could. I wanted them to fall back in love with each other. I wanted them to be happy.

Soon the hour would be over, and the six of us would sit at the rickety table in that small, hot kitchen and we'd eat. But while the food was wonderful, my mother and father hardly even looked at one another anymore and instead kept their attention on us, asking about school, about the tree fort my brother and I were building out in the woods, about the Beatles album my older sister listened to, the drawings my younger sister did each afternoon. We rarely left the table hungry, but there was a hollowness in the air, a dark unspeakable stillness, one my father would soon drive into, and away.

Sometimes when the husband leaves, his friends leave with him. That's what happened to my mother; Pop drove off early in late fall, our gravel driveway dusted with frost. He hugged us kids one at a time, tears in his eyes, and said he'd come see us in a few days, maybe take us out to eat; he was only living a few towns away. Then he drove down through the trees in his packed Lancer and was gone.

So too were his friends. And the parties. I don't know how long it was before my mother was able to buy a second car or got her first job waiting tables, or when exactly she began to go back to school, get her degree, and start working in social services. I do remember that we moved a lot, from one cheap rented house to the next. To be closer to Pop, we ended up in Massachusetts and lived in old mill towns along the Merrimack River in or near neighborhoods of tall weeds and trash, sagging porches that smelled like piss, stolen shopping carts lying on their sides that women would pick up and push to the grocery store once their welfare checks came in.

I got beat up a lot, and my brother and I started roaming the streets with a gang of kids with nothing better to do than steal and get high and look for day parties down in the projects. My older sister fell in with an older crowd, young men with beards and long ponytails who sold drugs and who rode up to our house on Harleys, parking in the scrappy lawn out front before they came in to get high in our living room and blast the stereo our mother's new boyfriend had bought us. My younger sister, Nicole, holed herself up in her room reading, writing, and doing her homework. She installed a padlock on her bedroom door and locked it whenever she was away from home.

These years, food was scarce. Even with my father's steady child support payments, my mother just didn't make enough to keep the fridge and cabinets stocked. It was hard enough keeping the rent paid on time, the electricity on, the heat filling the house through those endless winters. It was hard enough just to keep all four growing kids in at least one pair of pants, a shirt and sweater or two, and a pair of sneakers that might last a year. It was hard enough to keep her succession of used cars gassed up and running, though I don't believe she ever filled a tank; so many times she'd pull up to the pumps, dig through her purse for change, smile at the attendant, and ask for something like, "A dollar and fourteen cents' worth, please."

What money she did have budgeted for food went to meals she could cook quickly after she got home from work: canned soup or stew, macaroni and cheese, or the one we had most often, Frito Pie. Standing there in her earrings and work clothes—ironed pants and a blouse, maybe a bracelet around her wrist—she'd open a bag of Fritos, spread some out on the bottom of a casserole dish, then dump in two cans of Hormel chili, cover it with a layer of raw onions, more Fritos, and grated cheese. She'd bake this for thirty or forty minutes, the smell filling the downstairs like home cooking used to, and then we'd all grab a bowlful and eat in front of *The Waltons* or *All in the Family* or whatever it was we were watching.

Many nights she'd come home with grease-stained bags from McDonald's or Burger King, convenient meals she couldn't afford.

I was a teenager, so maybe I didn't know I missed how we all used to sit down each night and eat as a family, but my mother did; she suggested we start having sit-down breakfasts together, and she got up every weekday morning an hour earlier to pull that off. I had made a room for myself up in the attic. It wasn't heated, but it was away from everyone else, especially any of my sister's friends who might be showing up in the afternoons. I had a bed and a desk and a black light on the wall that lit up neon stars and planets I'd painted on the ceiling. I had my record player and fifteen Bob Dylan albums, music that reminded me of Pop, who used to play him a lot, too.

Lying in my bed in the early morning darkness, my breath clouding in front of me, I'd hear the door open at the bottom of the dusty stairwell and my mother's cheerful voice calling me down to breakfast. Eventually the five of us would be sitting at the dining room table we rarely used, the blue light of early morning seeping through the windows: Jeb with his wild hair and downy whiskers; Nicole in the brown sweater she wore all winter, partially hiding the brace she endured for her scoliosis; my older sister, Suzanne, in hip-hugger jeans and a T-shirt, black eyeliner around both eyes like bruises. Mom would be dressed for her job working down in Boston in the lead-paint poisoning prevention program, and I'd be there, too, my hair tied back in a long ponytail, hungry, grateful for this new thing Mom was trying.

Some mornings she'd serve us steaming bowls of oatmeal or Cream of Wheat with cinnamon toast—bread she'd butter then sprinkle with sugar and cinnamon and slide under the blue flames of the broiler; other mornings, it'd be buckwheat pancakes and hot bacon and real orange juice. One morning we woke to eggs Benedict with hollandaise sauce and baked peaches in pools of melted butter and caramelized brown sugar.

But this didn't last. It couldn't; we were kids who habitually went to bed late and had a hard time getting up in the morning. Before our mother started these breakfasts, she'd be on her way to work when we were supposed to leave the house to catch the bus around seven. Even with those wonderful smells filling the house once again, we rarely made it to the table, and my mother, depriving herself of a little extra sleep for this, gave up.

Most mornings, only Nicole would get up on time and walk herself to school a half mile north. Jeb, Suzanne, and I would sleep till we woke two or three hours later than we should have. Some days we'd stay home. Other days we'd go to school late, which meant a four-mile walk through town to the high school. I'm sure Suzanne and I walked together many days, but I remember more clearly doing it alone, walking across Main Street down into the avenues, streets of two- and three-decker row houses, a lot of them with Dobermans or German shepherds chained in their dirt yards. In some were babies' toys scattered among the dog shit, the dogs barking at me behind chain-link fences. I'd cut across Cedar down Sixth Avenue past the auto parts store and junkyard, the battered shells of cars sitting in the weeds, many of the windshields collapsed into the front seats, the rims rusted, the lug bolts like eyes staring out at me.

But those years I felt watched by no one. The weekday

mornings when we slept late and didn't go to school, our report cards showed this, sixty to eighty absences a year, dozens and dozens of marks for tardiness. What was strange is that no adult at school really seemed to notice too much. There'd be an occasional letter sent home to our mother, but the counselor or vice principal or whoever it was always wanted to meet during a weekday sometime. How could she do that? She had to work.

I'd make my way through town, past the boarded-up shops on Winter Street, the gas station and used car lot, the pizza shop and Dunkin' Donuts where on summer nights old men—Puerto Rican or Dominican—would sit in lawn chairs in the parking lot, smoking and talking and spitting.

At Railroad Square, I'd walk under the black iron trestle covered with hot-paint graffiti: Joey and Lisa 4-ever, Tommy loves Denise!, USMC Cpl. Steve L. RIP, U suck! On the sidewalk would be broken glass and cigarette butts, and I'd walk over them in the Dingo boots I wore because that's what all the toughest kids at the high school wore, the ones with long hair and a leather jacket like me, the ones who skipped classes and hung around behind the M and L wings selling J's and hits of brown mescaline, orange sunshine, and THC. Fastened to their belts were Buck knives in leather pouches they covered with their shirts, and maybe I thought if I looked like them, they'd leave me alone and I wouldn't have to fight for just looking at them a second too long. After a while it worked; because I looked like them, they didn't see me anymore. But the cops did. Especially those late weekday mornings walking through town when I should've been in algebra class, world history, gym; I'd pass more barrooms, a porn shop I never had the guts to walk into, St. Joe's

Catholic church, a cruiser pulling up and a cop yelling out at
me, "Why ain't you in school?"

"I had a doctor's appointment."

"Where's your parents?"

"Working."

"How'd you get to the doctor?"

"Walked."

"Well, keep walkin'." And he'd drive off in his police car,
his antenna swaying back and forth like a scolding finger.

I deserved a scolding, I knew that; I was undisciplined and
had no direction and got up each day with the desire simply
to get through it. I didn't know if my brother and sisters felt
the same way, but my mother seemed to; most weeknights,
she'd be stretched out on the floor in front of the TV asleep
in her work clothes by eight o'clock, my brother and sisters
and me free to do whatever we wanted, do homework or not
do homework, fight or ignore each other, ignore the five
days of dishes stacked in the kitchen sink and on the counters; ignore the overflowing garbage in the trash bucket or
the mountain of bags in the garage because none of us carried any out to the curb on garbage night; ignore the dirty
clothes hanging out of the full hampers in both bathrooms;
ignore the fact that we each did our own laundry when we
needed to, one at a time, going down to the basement and
putting into the machine one pair of underwear, a pair of
jeans, a pair of socks, a T-shirt and sweater, using an entire
water load, then drying this same outfit for an hour in the
dryer, each of us doing it this way, ignoring the others; ignore the dust everywhere, the loose hairs, the grit tracked
over the linoleum floors and throw-rugs; ignore that our
dog, Dirt, shat regularly up on the second floor hallway in

the dark corner near my door up to my attic bedroom; ignore that we could walk out of that house and not come home till midnight or later; ignore that we only saw our father on Sundays for dinner at a restaurant, that he never called us and we never called him; ignore that most nights my older sister would go up to her room with her boyfriend and smoke dope and listen to her albums; ignore that at fourteen I'd been seeing Debbie, black and sweet and shy with a soft voice and a mischievous giggle, and she and I would do it in my bed with no protection on a regular Tuesday or Wednesday night, the phony glow of black-lit planets and stars stuck to the ceiling above us.

Every few weeks it would all become just too much; my mother would start yelling and there'd be some changes: a new chore list; stricter rules on getting to school; and for a while she cooked more. But it was like living inside a great slumbering beast who'd woken just long enough to blink its watery eyes, howl, then turn over, and go back to sleep; we all fell once again into our solitary roles in this house with no head. We'd become a family in blood and name only.

But during these gray years, there were bright days my mother always rallied for, when she seemed to shrug off the massive weight that was raising children alone, and it was like watching a night-blooming flower open its petals in the gloom: holidays. For a while, they changed everything; she'd clean the house, and with genuine good cheer coax us into getting off our asses to clean, too. She'd put some Rolling Stones on the stereo and turn it up loud and make decorations out of construction paper and glue and yarn and glitter, taping these brilliant colors around the house. At Thanksgiving, there'd be earth tones—browns and greens and yellows. At Christmas: red, silver, and gold. On our birthdays we'd wake up to a pile of presents in the living room, each of them wrapped by her; sometimes the paper would be homemade, a grocery bag she'd stenciled stars onto then dressed with twine and a rope bow. There'd be store-bought paper, too, cut and taped perfectly around our new clothes, records, or books, these boxes laid out and stacked so that there always appeared to be more than there were. I'm convinced she spent the rent money on all this, that she put presents on layaway accounts she'd spend an entire year paying down. But that was beside the point for she was reminding us, and maybe herself, that life was meant to be more joyful and abundant than the one we had fallen into, that life was indeed a banquet, a grand carnival, the centerpiece of which was always food.

Thanksgiving and Christmas was one long meal of roast turkey stuffed with cornbread dressing; there'd be standing rib roast and ham and baked squash; there'd be Yorkshire pudding, homemade cranberry relish, steaming dirty rice and mashed potatoes and rolls made from scratch. On our birthdays, whether they fell on a weeknight or not, she'd still ask each of us what we wanted for our special meal, and she'd come home early and cook it.

But I'd begun to resist this tradition; it felt forced to me, slightly false, and I told Mom she could make whatever she wanted, I didn't care. I had a few friends by then and spent hours in the basement lifting weights and punching the heavy bag. I got to where I could do one thousand sit-ups without stopping, and on off days my friend Bill and I would run six to ten miles with seven-pound bars in our hands. Earlier that summer, visiting my mother's parents in Fishville, Louisiana, I'd cut off my ponytail.

At the time I thought I was training myself for the neighborhoods we lived in, but I was wrong; I was training for something else, for the day I could kick Suzanne's drug-dealing hoods out of the house myself, for the day I could lift my sleeping, overwhelmed mother up off the rug and carry her to bed and tuck her in like a child, for the day I could pull Nicole's padlock off her door and welcome her back with arms as big as a father's.

It was the second week of September, my sixteenth birthday, and I had a new family: Big Bill and crazy-eyed Leavitt, Roach and 260-pound Stevie B., slow-dancing Cheryl, Connie, and Effie. In a few weeks Roach would get stabbed at the high school, the blade of Cormier's Buck knife just missing his liver, and the rest of us would be hunting down Cormier for months, him and any of his friends, but I didn't know this then. All I knew is that it was only four-thirty and Mom was already home from work. She looked tired, her eyes a bit bloodshot, and she was unloading two bags of groceries in the kitchen, smiling at me as I came in. The morning had been too rushed for presents, and she asked me if I wanted them before my meal or after.

"I don't care."

"Well, I do."

"After, then."

She pulled out a plump roast, pink and tied off and wrapped in plastic. She raised her eyebrows and looked genuinely happy. "I'm making your meal."

I nodded; even now, when I didn't ask for one, it's what she cooked for me, the one I'd always asked for when I was small.

"Pop coming?"

"Six o'clock." She poured olive oil in a black skillet and lit the burner beneath it. She opened the cupboard and brought down the bag of flour, dumping some into a mixing bowl. She pinched in salt, pepper, and paprika, then she unwrapped the roast and pushed it into the flour, covering and patting it till it was coated white. She turned on the oven and when the olive oil was just beginning to smoke, she lowered the meat into it, making it pop and sizzle. I knew after she'd browned it she would roast the meat in the oven and from its drippings she would make the gravy, and I turned and left the kitchen then; it was like being too close to the source of something mysterious I'd come to count on, and I didn't want to know how she did it.

I walked up the two flights of stairs for my room. It was one of those odd afternoons when all of us were home and nobody else. My sister Nicole had left her bedroom door open and lay on her bed reading, her scoliosis brace pushing against her chin. Suzanne's door was open too, and I looked in and saw she was writing something in a notebook, a letter maybe? Homework? From down the hall I could hear my brother practicing his guitar, classical guitar he'd begun to teach himself; months later he would play something for us called a Bach Prelude, and we would look at each other, blinking in wonder.

In my room I changed into my sweats and a T-shirt. Something loud drove fast down Main Street, and I glanced out the window but saw only the broad leaves of our oak tree, fading from green to yellow. At the basement door, I watched my mother open the jar of dried rice. She'd put some jazz on the stereo, something with a lot of piano in it, and the kitchen smelled like meat smoke and hot oil. She turned and smiled at me. "Workin' out?"

"Just a short one." And I hurried down the worn stairs, ducking under the dust-webbed plumbing into the room where six days a week I was trying to carve myself into something hard.

But lying down on the bench, my heart was beating faster than it should, and I could pretend I didn't care, but I knew it was from hope, hope that my mother's boyfriend would be staying at his house tonight, hope that Suzanne would stick around and Nicole would come down out of her room and Jeb would, too, hope that Pop was leaving his small apartment across the river right now, climbing into his Lancer and driving the three miles to our house where I'd meet him at the door, sweating and breathing hard, the veins showing in my new muscles, and it didn't matter if he had a present for me or if there were any presents at all; I wanted him to go into the kitchen and sip a Jim Beam with Mom, jazz playing, the entire house filling with the smells of my meal.

And soon enough we'd all be sitting down to it, lighted candles in the center of the table, the silverware matching. Mom would sit at one end, still young really, still beautiful, her fresh lipstick catching some of the candlelight. Pop would be at the other, his hair thinner and combed back, his beard trimmed, his eyes shining as he looked over his four teenage children: Suzanne with her black eyeliner and brushed hair; Nicole in her brace that made her sit too straight; Jeb and the far-off fire in his eyes, the new calluses on his fingertips; and me in a tight T-shirt pretending I wasn't trying to show my muscles every time I moved, pretending I didn't notice the six of us were all in this one room at the same time, sitting together again, eating together again.

Pop would lift his Jim Beam and make a birthday toast. Love would glint in his eyes, love for us all, Mom included, and we'd tap our glasses and sip. Then we'd begin to talk over each other, passing around the platter of sliced roast and the bowl of steaming white rice, the spoonfuls of green peas, the tin of homemade rolls with butter. There'd be fresh sliced pears over a bed of lettuce, and German chocolate cake for later, but right now we'd be saving the most important part for last—Mom's gravy, that thick, dark, salt and meat-drippings gravy that covered everything, that made everything taste whole, that seemed to flow into the meal and through it, like blood.

# Food Envy

## Aimee Bender

## I.

MY FAVORITE FOOD HAS ALWAYS BEEN OTHER PEOPLE'S FOOD.

This attitude is, more or less, limited to food. I don't covet celebrity dresses while gazing mournfully into my closet. I've never been a boyfriend-thief. As a teenager, it was okay that the popular girls had big blue eyes and I didn't. But if Dori brought that squished tuna-fish salad sandwich with sweet relish on Weber's bread to lunch during high school? I could hardly *stand* it. Every day, I'd stare at her lunch bag the way another girl watches her crush flirting across the quad, and if Dori pulled out that plastic baggie with those easily identifiable pressed white triangles, I'd use whatever means necessary to get a taste: pathetic sad-eyed doggie looks, direct bartering, friend favors, compliments, money, whatever.

"I mean, could I just have one bite?" I'd ask, in the

wheedling indirect voice of the teenage girl, and generous
Dori would hand over her sandwich triangle, resigned. We'd
been friends for years. She ate that tuna all the time, but still,
I'm sure it was grating to have to deal with my rays of desper-
ation on her right side, rays that focused only on the sandwich and not really much on the human interaction that
framed the sandwich. The sandwich was so good, though:
light tuna, not albacore, just the right amount of mayonnaise, chopped egg white, a dash of sweet relish, mixed until
spreadable and then applied thinly on the soft processed
bread I never got at home. And, for the final selling point,
the pièce de résistance, it was all slightly squished down as if
it had been lightly hammered or pressed. That part sounds a
little gross, and was probably due to backpacks and travel
time, but the pressing made it taste so much better. It was so
very, very eatable.

"Aimee, you're such a mooch," my friends would say, on
occasion, and I would laugh and ignore it, because I had no
intention of changing and I just hoped to God they would
continue to tolerate and feed me.

Due to a limited allowance, I'd rarely buy school food, but
if someone else happened to get one of the doughy squares of
cafeteria pizza? I would ache for a bite, fixated on the electric
orange tomato sauce as it soaked into the bread. The giant
chocolate chip cookies with half-baked interiors? Would
take over my mind.

On the occasion that I did buy one of those cookies, it
never looked as good as my neighbor's. And certainly mine
was always gone way before my neighbor's. How could people eat so slowly?

I hardly starved at home: many times, my mother sent me

to school with hefty sandwiches on challah bread, rare roast beef and tomatoes and green leafy lettuce. (Often an effective barter for Dori's tuna.) She bought mostly health food, preferring to shop at an upscale market in Brentwood, a wealthy suburb of Los Angeles, occasionally spotting movie stars in the aisles. But you cannot anticipate where deprivation settles itself. I held myself back in so many ways at that age: I couldn't really decide what subjects I liked or didn't like, and sports were hard, and I didn't know how to talk to other people very well, and the only boys I could let myself have big crushes on were the ones who would never ever go out with me. And as for sex, that was too scary for me. Food was the main place I could settle all my desire, and that is a whole lot of longing to put on one chocolate chip cookie.

## II.

It began years before. In third grade, a girl named Su Lin Woo entered the classroom halfway through the year. Her family had recently emigrated from China, and she was low-key and nice, with a slight accent and a likably nerdy manner. I was a third-grader in a class of mixed grades, and I had taken it upon myself to be something of an older sister to anyone new, so I probably showed Su Lin Woo where to store her workbook, introduced her around the tables, tried to make her feel welcome. Su Lin was a fairly neutral class member; she did fine with her schoolwork, and was cordial to most everyone. She was neither show-off nor wallflower. Together, we learned our irregular verbs, drew pictures of narwhals, and played Uno in the carpeted library corner if we finished early.

One lunch time, a bunch of us were sitting together in the cafeteria, at a dough-colored table in front of a mural of a dancing banana and an apple cored by a friendly worm tipping its top hat. I was eating a peanut butter sandwich— which was all I ate in grade school—when Su Lin opened up her lunch box and removed from it a tinfoil packet, neatly folded into a square. Even her tinfoil seemed special; it looked like it had been ironed. The panels shone with a dull elegance, crinkling at the corners. My curiosity was piqued, instantly.

"What's that?" I asked.

With careful fingers, she opened the top of the foil, and sitting inside were three rice balls. About the size of golf balls. They were delicately packed down, and appeared to be lightly salted. Homemade care wafted from each grain.

"Rice balls," she said, indicating the trio.

"What are rice balls?"

"Would you like to try?"

As I said, I was a very picky eater in grade school. If the apple in my bag had a bruise, I'd toss it into the trash can with the carefree ignorance of a girl who had never traveled far beyond her home of American privilege.

Still, I was intrigued by the look of that rice ball. A few other kids finished up and ran off to play Four Square.

"Okay," I said.

Su Lin handed one over, onto my napkin. I put my sandwich away. My hands grew nervous. What if I didn't like it? Would I be able to hand it back? Was that rude? Could I crab-walk over to the bathroom so she wouldn't see and spit it into the sink? What if I was allergic to it? Would I die? Would Su Lin ever speak to me again if I threw it up all over the dough-colored table?

I watched as she picked one up herself, with her fingers, neatly. Mirroring her actions, I bit inside. The rice itself was perfectly taut, even a little sticky, and the saltiness was deeply satisfying. Was it my imagination, or did it still taste warm? Something about it soothed me. Something about the balance of ingredients, and the obvious care that had been taken in making it. On the third bite, like a gustatory Cortés, I discovered a tiny portion of salted chopped meat at the center. Thrilling! The meat was tasty and lean—probably beef or pork. And modestly applied: there were two bites of meat at most, which suited my own tentative nature about food in those days. I ate the rest of that rice ball as slowly as I could, and thanked Su Lin Woo over and over, telling her how wonderful it was, how different, how delicious, how special. I told her to thank her mom, too. I wished, briefly, for my own tinfoil packet someday, with my name written on it in Chinese, and those pearls inside, all for me.

That day, I sat with Su Lin instead of going to Four Square as she finished her food at her own gentle pace. I always enjoyed her company, but to be honest, I stayed there mostly in hopes that she would give me one more bite. She finished the first rice ball. She finished the second. She folded the tinfoil into a square and smiled at me. Even at eight years old, she knew she had given more than enough.

We watched our friends throw the red rubber ball at each other.

Su Lin was an upstanding sharer; even at that age, she did not use the rice balls as a popularity bid, or as leverage of any kind. The next time they showed up in her lunch, out of fairness, she gave the third rice ball to little Fairuza, or to sporty Missy, who each enjoyed it thoroughly, even though in my heart of hearts I believed no one could appreciate that rice ball as much as I could.

This was over twenty-five years ago and I *still* remember them. Why? Was it because I knew that once Su Lin left the third grade, I would never taste them again? I've searched menus at Chinese restaurants, but I believe this particular rice ball was a Woo specialty. Eating them was like visiting a country with a specialty visa; I got to go to Su Lin's land three times, and after that, the taste was only a memory, impossible to revisit.

Sure enough, by fourth grade, all of us changed to different classrooms, and Su Lin and her food were gone. I looked her up recently in an old photo album, and there she is, wearing glasses and an old patterned shirt from the 1970s, hair straight with a tiny flip up at the ends. A friendly smile.

Food made by friends' parents came with a tinge of melancholy, and maybe that is part of why it tasted so good. This was the bread and butter of their world, one I could never be a real part of; I could get a taste of life in Su Lin Woo's house, even though I never visited, and I envied that mysterious and therefore perfect world beyond. Where love was as easy and simple as the taut warmth of the rice, folded into a tinfoil treasure packet. Su Lin's world was foreign to me, which was exciting, but Dori's was foreign, too; her tuna sandwich felt like a little piece of joyous Americana, a mayonnaisian indicator of a larger Rockwellian whole, and I imagined, in both scenes, the families sitting around, eating their tuna sandwiches or their rice balls, singing songs in front of a fire. I loved those items because they were unattainable even as I was eating them: they evoked a hunger much larger than actual hunger, and in each bite, held the bittersweetness of a kiss between lovers who meet while traveling and who will part on the dock of a port, never to see each other again.

## III.

I wrote Dori an e-mail and asked for her mom's tuna-fish recipe. So, courtesy of Dori and Cindy Rosenthal, here it is:

- Starkist chunk light tuna (which—as a side benefit—has less mercury than albacore)

- Hard-boiled egg, white only, no yolk. Two eggs per one can of tuna.

- Best Foods mayonnaise (regular, not light or fat-free)

- Pickle relish—Del Monte?—enough to taste and look evenly sprinkled with green.

- Put it all in a round wooden bowl with a round knife and chop it all up, and then spread it on bread.

- Cut into triangles.

My addition: press the bread down lightly with the pads of fingertips.

I have no way of contacting Su Lin Woo.

## IV.

I became partially cured of my food envy when I taught elementary school in San Francisco. The lunchroom was a busy, rowdy place, and the kids ran in, yelling, after class, and with grubby hands, pulled mini miracles from their brown sack lunches: soft bologna sandwiches, handfuls of crisp Fritos, leftover pizza, even homemade sushi. I sat above them, watching for fights and hurt feelings, and I could feel the familiar itching begin in my chest as the students undid the plastic holding their salami sandwiches together. I embarrassed myself, with that desire.

Most of us teachers at this school were in our early twenties, and we were enthusiastic, anxious, long-haired, mostly women, wearing funky goth shoes and conservative blouses, trying not to say *fuck* or *kick ass* in front of the children. Unlike the structured schooltime that had shaped our lives so far, here we were, on our own, making money, living somewhere near the Outer Sunset district of San Francisco, not going to classes but teaching them instead.

One afternoon, when I was on lunch duty, Yuri, one of the many Russian students who lived in the neighborhood, pulled out a piroshki, a delightful-looking fried bread item with meat tucked inside. A kind of Russian rice ball. Homemade.

He unwrapped it with careful hands, and explained to me what it was.

"Ms. Bender," he said, "this is a famous Russian food."

Then he took a big, happy bite. It did not cross his mind to offer, and it shouldn't have. This was his lunch, and I was his teacher, and I had my own lunch, some kind of blah turkey sandwich on wheat, which actually I had already enjoyed, and I wasn't even hungry. The previous week, I'd had to listen to myself ask six-year-old freckled Andrea for one barbecue-flavored potato chip, please? and the open-minded but bewildered look on her face as she held out the crinkly Baggie for her teacher had shamed me. Awful. The itch in my chest was intense, but I just watched as Yuri ate his whole piroshki, smiling as he chewed. "It has meat in the middle," he said.

One of the long-haired goth-shoed teachers had recently been fired for sifting through the kids' lunches while they were in class. She had snuck into a Baggie and taken a big bite of a peanut butter sandwich. Somehow, she had been caught. Probably one of the kids started crying when she saw what was left of her lunch; maybe there was even a telltale stain of red lipstick on the bread. The whole thing was pretty ludicrous—eating the sandwiches of first-graders—but I understood. How hard it was, to be faced with those bags of parental care, row after row after row, while we were in our early twenties, struggling with who we were becoming. How hard it is, just to deal with the lunch that you have.

Yuri finished his piroshki and brought out a very fishy-smelling sandwich on rye, with silvery scales poking out the back of the bread.

"Herring is delicious, too," he said, grinning at me, biting in.

The itch dissolved. Sometimes, at least, I caught a break.

# Stir Gently and Serve

## Jane Stern

I HAVE ALWAYS LOVED THANKSGIVING. I AM A GREAT FAN OF turkey and gravy and stuffing and pumpkin pies and I have even grown to love the unlovable Thanksgiving staples of creamed onions and Brussels sprouts. Thanksgiving is one of the stranger holidays because it doesn't involve the giving of presents, although to me a full plate of turkey and all the trimmings is about the greatest gift of all.

I grew up having Thanksgiving at my uncle Henry's house. He lived with my aunt Liz and their two children, Eric and Willa, in New Haven, Connecticut. Being a New York City child, I found everything about their house a wonder. The porch never failed to astound me, because even the richest people in Manhattan didn't have one, and located on the porch was one of the greatest of all things: a green vinyl hassock whose top opened to reveal a wealth of comic books:

Little Iodine, Millie the Model, Archie and Superman, girl, boy, and dog.

I was the youngest of all the cousins of my generation, and also an only child. This created a strange gestalt (a word I use as homage to Uncle Henry, who was a psychiatrist). When I was taken by my parents to my relatives' house I got to interact with other kids. I say *interact* rather than *play* because Eric, ten years older than I, was hardly interested in playing with a little girl with braids and a party dress, and Willa, who was fourteen years old to my ten, was such a glamorous teenager that all I could do was sit back and stare with wonder at her breasts and acne.

It seemed that the smell of cooking turkey exacerbated family dynamics so everyone was at their very best and very worst. This was not a bad thing in a family of histrionic Russian Jews, because we knew a thing or two about over-the-top drama. Our ancestors included the Tomaschevsky family, royalty of the Lower East Side's Yiddish Theater. My uncle Henry could have been a mopey Jewish Macbeth, my mother always spoke with the volume of Ethel Merman on stage, Aunt Liz was the reigning beauty, and my father had a steel plate in his head; must I really say more? The meal was interrupted every fifteen minutes by someone reading a poem or a complicated passage from Shakespeare or blasting a sad Joan Baez ballad from the record player. I don't remember anyone ever saying a prayer or offering a blessing, but we all waited for our turn to hog the spotlight.

I especially remember one Thanksgiving in 1958 at Uncle Henry's house. My grandmother was in top form, running around the table holding her trusty pink enema bag, making proclamations about turkey being constipating. Cousin Willa was having a complete emotional meltdown because all the grown-ups had disrespectfully called Elvis Presley "Elvis the Pelvis." My father was launching one of his diatribes about how shrinks were dangerous quacks in earshot of Uncle Henry, and Eric refused to come in from the driveway, where he was shooting baskets with a cigarette dangerously dangling from his bottom lip and mumbling to no one in particular about his hero, Lenny Bruce.

Somehow in the middle of these psychodramas my aunt Liz always produced the best dinner on the planet. While we were all in the dining room having our star turn on the family stage, she stayed in the kitchen fussing about. You could have placed lit matches under her fingernails and she would not have told you the secret of her stuffing, not because she was small-minded. More likely, she didn't know. She was a pinch-of-this-and-a-squirt-of-that sort of cook. To this day her stuffing remains, in my mind, the Platonic ideal. It was a simple formula, it had no exotic elements like sausage or chestnuts; it was just seasoned bread, but there was never a scrap left in the bowl at the end of the meal.

Certainly nothing on the table was up to current gourmet standards. The turkey was not deep-fried or brined. I am sure it was a Butterball or something like it, frozen solid as a rock at the local supermarket until its overnight swim in the kitchen sink. The bright red cranberry sauce was jelled and came directly out of the can. If you looked closely you could still see the ring of the can marks and even the date stamped on the bottom. The bread was some sort of soft supermarket rolls, and the pies and cakes were bought by my parents at one of the then-numerous West Side German-American Jewish bakeries. We always had one truly vile thing that no one ate, yet was always served for dessert. It was a kind of huge monster-like cream puff called a Nesselrode that featured handfuls of sickeningly sweet candied fruits cut up into tiny squares. It was disgusting but it was tradition, and so we counted on it being there every year.

Sadly, by the time I was twenty-five years old all my relatives except Eric had died, both of my parents and Uncle Henry and Willa from cancer, and Aunt Liz from Alzheimer's. But I had Michael, and Michael had a slew of relatives, too. We tried driving out to Chicago for the holiday meal, but it was never as satisfying as Thanksgiving with Uncle Henry. Unlike my tradition-bound and nutty family, the Sterns proved to be experimental. One Thanksgiving the Cuisinart had just come on the market and Michael's mother had puréed the entire meal. Another Thanksgiving was spent at the rich aunt and uncle's house where we ate capon (!) instead of turkey and were instructed to remove our shoes so that we wouldn't damage the polished wooden floors beneath our feet. We were told that the family dog had been given away because his toenails had been too scratchy.

Back in New Haven, Michael and I lived in a rental apartment across the street from where Uncle Henry and family had lived. It was strange to look out the window and see the familiar old white colonial and know that other people occupied the rooms. I wondered what would happen if I showed up for Thanksgiving. I spied on them from our apartment window. They appeared to be a family whose father, like my uncle Henry, taught at Yale. Like Uncle Henry he wore blue blazers and gray slacks when he left for work. I wondered if they ever ate Nesselrode, or if they had changed the great faded wallpaper in the dining room that featured Chinese sailing ships, but I was too shy even to ring the doorbell and introduce myself.

Michael and I were married in October 1970, and the calendar declared that Thanksgiving was just a month away. I decided that the only way to reclaim my family history and to get a satisfactory meal on Thanksgiving was to cook it myself. I knew that to replicate the family experience I would have to have at least a dozen people at the table, and I spent the better part of the week on the telephone, only to realize the hard fact that virtually everyone in America goes home for Thanksgiving, and those I called were not about to abandon their relatives for me.

But I persevered and finally found two sad sacks with nowhere to go. Michael was very interested in old movies, and these two guys were his film buddies. All three could tell you the name of the lighting man on a lesser Mitchell Leisen movie. They were such nerds (not my Michael, of course) that probably their families breathed a sigh of relief when they got another invitation to a Thanksgiving dinner.

We lived in a tiny one-bedroom apartment in a brownstone building overhanging one of the more busy exits of I-95. The kitchen was doll-size; the oven had probably never seen anything but a TV dinner.

I calculated that for four people a thirty-five-pound turkey would do. A thirty-five-pound turkey is approximately the size of a bear cub. I called in the order to the meat market down the block that had a sign in the window saying CALL IN TURKEY ORDERS. The night before Thanksgiving day I was given this HUGE wrapped package to take home. Not only would it not fit in any pan (of the two we owned) but the damn thing would not fit in the oven. I wanted Michael to trust my homemaking skills, so when he was out walking Richard, our bulldog, I took a big kitchen knife and hacked the hell out of the thing, whittling it down to a size that fit in a pan. I threw the bag with the neck and giblets in the garbage with three quarters of the raw turkey, and I covered what was left with aluminum foil in a makeshift roasting pan so things looked semi-normal.

You may have figured this out by now: I had no idea how to cook anything. I knew what was supposed to be included in the meal but had never made any of it. So the day before the holiday I had hit the supermarket, trying to find cans and boxes with labels that said how things were made. Obviously a cookbook was not a concept I understood at that point.

Here is what I made:

### Appetizers

Salami cornucopias (Wrap a circle of salami around a smear of cream cheese and a little piece of pickle, and spear with a toothpick. Found this on a salami package.)

Chopped liver on Ritz crackers (Because my parents always served this.)

Schmaltz herring (Ditto.)

Dry-roasted peanuts (Uncle Henry's favorites.)

Manhattans made from bottled Manhattan mix with maraschino cherries (Also a Henry thing.)

### Entrées

A huge thawed turkey hacked into unrecognizable pieces

3 large cans of Franco-American beef gravy (I didn't know they made turkey flavor.)

### Side Dishes

1 large bag of Pepperidge Farm stuffing mixed with tap water (Forgot to get the egg and any other things like celery or broth.)

Veg-All (Prison-like canned mixed vegetables.)

Instant mashed potatoes made with tap water (Because I forgot the butter and milk.)

Two cans of yams and two bags of miniature marshmallows

Cheap supermarket rolls (Forgot butter.)

Stouffer's frozen spinach soufflé (Michael's mother's standby.)

Frozen peas

### Desserts

Homemade pumpkin pie

Homemade apple pie

Neapolitan ice cream loaf (Sort of like a Nesselrode.)

Cool Whip (thawed)

Maraschino cherries

Taster's Choice instant coffee

Now, you might say that is a lot of food for four people. You also might say that it sounds utterly disgusting. You would be right on both counts. But as vile as the menu was, I figured it had to be good because it was a ton of work: shopping, mixing, chopping, heating up, stirring, simmering, stuffing, et cetera, none of which I had the slightest idea how to do. The best things were dumped out of cans; the worst things, like the cooked-from-scratch turkey and the homemade pies, were fiascos in the making. I had no kitchen utensils other than a fork and spoon, so the crusts for the pies and the yam casserole were made by the same technique with which cavemen cooked a million years back. I used my hands. Things got dropped on the floor and things got put back into casserole dishes. The foods were either as salty as a deer lick, or so bland even Squanto, the Native American who showed the Pilgrims how to celebrate Thanksgiving, would have run screaming.

But if there is one thing I am, it is prompt; and by five p.m., when Film Nerd Number One knocked on the door, I was ready to serve. Michael had been banished from the house for the day so I could do my cooking in peace. Nerd Number Two arrived at the same time as Michael and looked really happy to be invited. The air smelled like turkey cooking, and the table set with mismatched dishes and paper napkins looked as good as it ever had.

Michael poured the bottled Manhattans and the salami cornucopias were actually being eaten with gusto. There was one clear moment of feeling that I had done it. I was now a grown-up and the mantle of Thanksgiving had fallen on my capable shoulders.

It was time to put the meal on the table. In our utility-size kitchen I wrestled the partial turkey onto a platter. Everything else was plunked into bowls and containers. The meal took up most of the table; in fact, there was nowhere to sit. "I guess we will do this buffet style," Michael said, and nobody looked averse. Michael bounced around, giving me little pats and hugs. It is true that the way to a man's heart is through his stomach. The smell of roasting meat is better than any sexy perfume. "What a feast," Michael said with great enthusiasm as I handed him the electric knife we had received as a wedding gift.

In a few minutes Michael had hacked away at the turkey,

which was half cooked in some places and dry as Kleenex in others. "Let's eat!" he declared, and swiveled around to show me his handiwork.

"Jane?" he called out and looked at our guests in puzzlement. "Jane?" he tried again. No answer.

Our apartment consisted of a living room and an adjoining bedroom. There was no door, just a curtain we had tacked up between the rooms bordello style to give some semblance of privacy. He walked to the curtain and pulled it aside. I was there, in the bed, under a blanket, dead asleep.

Michael walked over and shook me. "What's the matter?" he asked. "Are you sick?"

"Nooooo . . . I'm just so tired," I said back in a tiny voice. "You start eating and I'll be there in five minutes."

Gamely Michael walked back to the living room, where our nerdish friends were heaping plates with what passed for Thanksgiving dinner. Michael joined them.

The next thing I knew it was ten p.m. Michael was washing the dishes in the kitchen sink and putting some of the food in the small refrigerator. He had put a dish of turkey on the floor for Richard, our bulldog, who sniffed a few times and walked away.

This was a terrible insult, given that Richard had no problem eating fountain pens and his own shit. How bad a cook was I?

When I woke up I felt more as if I was waking up from surgery than from sleep. I felt drugged and logy. "When did they leave?" I croaked.

"They left about an hour ago," Michael said, without lifting his head from looking at the dishes.

"What did you tell them?" I asked, suddenly self-conscious.

"I told them you fell asleep," Michael said. "What else could I tell them?"

"What did they say?" I continued.

"Nothing, they ate a lot and then we talked about movies," Michael said. Finally he faced me. He looked sad. "Why did you fall asleep?" he asked, wondering the same thing I did.

It wasn't until years later that I could answer the question. It had nothing to do with hours of cooking or the fabled L-tryptophan in turkey. Celebrating Thanksgiving without my family was a rite of passage, a crisis rite. With every stir of the spoon and ladle of gravy I was saying good-bye to what I had known, and reinventing a new path for myself. It did not matter if the food was good or bad. What mattered was that traditions would go on despite the chill of death. I did not have a family anymore but I was a family, at least to Michael and an ungrateful bulldog. In cooking the meal I had done the emotional equivalent of running a marathon. And like marathon runners who drop to their knees as soon as they cross the finish line, I had collapsed.

It was a wise move to invite such undemanding guests. They apparently were happy as clams because there was food on the table and someone to analyze Roger Corman movies with. Michael, looking back, enjoyed a rare Thanksgiving without the Sturm und Drang of family feasts.

In the years to follow we chose not to celebrate with what remaining family we had scattered around the country. We chose to be Thanksgiving outlaws, to do odd things like go to the local diner for hot turkey sandwiches, or buy a huge tub of candy and sit in an empty movie theater watching the show. Sometimes we accepted friends' invitations and we would take a dish or two. It was interesting but not intimate to be asked to other people's homes for the holidays. We were not too proud to shun offers of leftovers to take home; we took as much as they gave us.

On those occasions, while driving back home to our house in Connecticut, where we moved a few years after the New Haven apartment, we would look through the picture windows and see families clustered together at the table. The interior lights glowed golden in the crisp fall air. I was once one of them, on the other side of the frosted windows, but not now.

# Surf and Turf

## Richard Russo

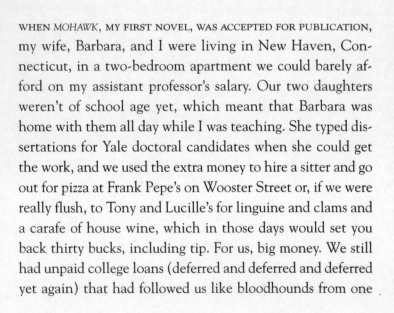

WHEN MOHAWK, MY FIRST NOVEL, WAS ACCEPTED FOR PUBLICATION, my wife, Barbara, and I were living in New Haven, Connecticut, in a two-bedroom apartment we could barely afford on my assistant professor's salary. Our two daughters weren't of school age yet, which meant that Barbara was home with them all day while I was teaching. She typed dissertations for Yale doctoral candidates when she could get the work, and we used the extra money to hire a sitter and go out for pizza at Frank Pepe's on Wooster Street or, if we were really flush, to Tony and Lucille's for linguine and clams and a carafe of house wine, which in those days would set you back thirty bucks, including tip. For us, big money. We still had unpaid college loans (deferred and deferred and deferred yet again) that had followed us like bloodhounds from one end of the country to the other, and our car was so old the thieves that roamed Whalley Avenue and the Boulevard at night had stopped breaking into it. In other words, publication and the advance against royalties that publication would bring were welcome.

You want to experience joy in its purest form? Here's what you do. Stand in front of a freshman composition class and explain that you won't be able to meet them next Tuesday because you're taking the train into the city to meet with your editor. When you've done that, tell the chair of your department. Tell anyone who asks if you'll be able to attend a meeting that Tuesday, "Sorry, I can't. I have to take the train into the city to meet my editor." If someone wants you to attend a meeting on, say, Wednesday, you reply, "Sorry, I can't. No wait, I can. It's *Tuesday* that I'm taking the train into the city to meet my editor." Is there a more glorious sentence in the English language? Each phrase—*take the train . . . into the city . . . meet my editor*—so magical, so full of Cheever and Fitzgerald. Not New York City, *the* city. Saying such a sentence out loud is like having sex that first time; you just know you'll never tire of it.

Barbara, whose birthday was in a few days, had never even visited New York (having grown up in Tucson), so I was anxious to show her around, this despite the fact that I'd only been there a couple of times myself since I was a kid and had seen little more than the packed elevators and beige corridors of MLA convention hotels. The actual advance from my publisher hadn't arrived yet, but we knew it was coming, so we felt justified in plundering our anemic savings. In fact, we left just enough in the account to keep it open. I wanted to make sure we had enough cash to cover taxis and two good meals; our sole credit card would be of no use, maxed out as usual, with not even enough leeway to charge a pair of socks.

We had lunch at the Top of the Sixes, the only restaurant I knew of with the requisite loft for the occasion. We arrived without reservations but I must have looked to the maître d' like a man who'd just sold a novel, because he took us to a table at the window with sweeping views of Manhattan. Sitting there, we couldn't help but feel we'd turned a corner. The people at the next table were speaking rapid French, for god's sake, though the only word we were able to pick out was *Bloomingdale's*. We both ordered pan-seared scallops, which our waiter informed us were served rare unless we objected—in which event, his manner implied, he would think less of us. We did not want that and so said that of course, rare scallops would be fine with us. They came three to a plate, which would have been disappointing had they not been the size of filet mignons. They'd been in a pan, and recently, but not for long. They wiggled like Jell-O beneath our forks and were ice cold in the center, but they tasted like scallops taste when you've just taken the train into the city to meet with your editor and you're eating them fifty floors up. Damn good. I was about to say to Barbara, "These are damn good," when I happened to notice a man come out onto the roof a couple stories below, where he unzipped and arced his yellow stream into the street below, proving, as life will, that nothing ever comes to you clean. I glanced over at my wife to see if she'd noticed the man and saw that she'd stopped chewing.

## Surf

**INGREDIENTS:** olive oil, scallops, the juice of one lemon, a pan.

**PROCEDURE:** Put a little olive oil in the bottom of a pan over very high heat. You're looking for that magical moment just before the oil begins to scorch and you have to throw it out. In other words, really, really hot. You're going to sear the scallops, not cook them. Once you put the scallops in the pan, *don't mess with them.* Let them bond with the pan at the molecular level for one minute, tops, then turn them over. If they stick, good. Find a way to unstick them and sear the other side for forty-five seconds. Add the lemon juice. Fifteen seconds later remove the scallops. Lower the heat a bit and reduce the pan juices until the liquid resembles thirty-weight motor oil in terms of consistency, drizzle it over the scallops, and you're good to go. Serve with something that goes well with scallops. (This may or may not be the way scallops are prepared at the Top of the Sixes.)

Which brings us to Turf. Now I *do* realize that in some restaurants Surf and Turf will be steak and lobster, or steak and jumbo shrimp, but for us it was steak and scallops and we ate them about six hours apart in different restaurants that day in New York. Some restaurants actually serve them together as part of the same meal, but I'm just telling you how we did it.

The other restaurant I was determined to take Barbara to was a legendary steak house, a hangout for famous writers, editors, athletes, and celebrities. I couldn't recall its name, but back in grad school my writing mentor was always telling us stories about the place where his agent, also something of a legend, took all his clients and, when the meal was finished, *signed for it.* "Imagine," Bob, my mentor, said. "All the other dick-swingers at nearby tables are pulling out their gold and platinum credit cards, but this guy just signs the bottom of the check." It had been a while since I'd spoken to Bob, so I called and told him I was going to be in the city and what was the name of that great steak house he used to rave about, the one where his agent just signed the bottom of the check. He told me the name, adding, "and it ain't cheap," no doubt remembering me from the days when we grad students congregated at a local campus dive after our Thursday workshop and tossed coins and the odd crumpled dollar bill into the center of the table in hopes that they'd add up to the price of a pitcher of cheap beer. When he asked what I was going to be doing in the city, I had no choice but to tell him.

Having been warned, I should have glanced at the menu posted on the wall outside the restaurant. My thinking was, this was a street-level type restaurant. It couldn't be as expensive as the Top of the Sixes.

"Uh . . . ," my wife said, when we were seated and she'd opened her menu.

"Yes," I agreed. "You're right."

"Can we?"

"Just about."

"You think?"

"Just . . . about," I said, doing some arithmetic in my head. Just about. If we didn't order appetizers. Or side dishes. Or anything to drink. And if we tipped fifteen percent rather than the twenty demanded, I knew, by New York waiters. I resisted the impulse to pull out my wallet to make sure. I did, however, pat my shirt pocket to make sure I still had our return train tickets.

"Our beef is aged and served medium rare," our tuxedoed

waiter informed us helpfully, and we agreed that this was the proper way to treat an aged steak. Barbara normally ordered her steaks medium, but having declined the offer of appetizers, we were both anxious to get back into the man's good graces if possible. "And what else can I bring you? The creamed spinach is excellent."

"No, nothing else," I said, trying to sound jaunty.

"*Just* the steaks, then?" he said, rather louder than was absolutely necessary, I thought, the tables being so close together.

"Just," I said, even jauntier, nearly adding the phrase, "my good man."

"Just whatever normally comes with the meal," my wife clarified hopefully.

What came with our steaks was a sprig of parsley. The curly kind.

## Turf

INGREDIENTS: you will need two steaks (I don't recommend aging them at home, and the ones aged in the supermarket beyond their sell-by dates are different, I'm told, than steaks aged in dry meat lockers), a fire, an oven preheated to 450 degrees, and two extra-large plates.

PROCEDURE: Your steaks should be thick and round, like a baseball, so that it's not immediately apparent which side should go on the grill. To ensure a char, your fire should be very hot. Turn your steaks over when it seems like a good idea to do so and char the other side. Take them off the grill while they still wiggle like raw scallops and pop them in the oven. There your steaks will plump, whereas continued grilling will result in shrinkage; the idea is to trick yourself into believing that the steak you're eating is bigger than it is. How long you leave it in the oven will depend on how big the steak really is. Don't worry, you're probably going to ruin four or five before you get the timing right. The extra-large plate is to emphasize the fact that you're not having a baked potato or any creamed spinach. A very small sprig of parsley also helps in this respect.

After a fine meal, my wife and I always enjoy a walk. Our steak house was located in the theater district, which meant a walk of about twenty-five blocks to Grand Central Station, and it wouldn't have been unpleasant at all but for the rain and the fact that we'd not thought to bring an umbrella. My own spirits couldn't have been higher. That afternoon my editor had told me he thought I'd written a very fine novel indeed. Better yet, he expressed every confidence that I had other good novels in me. I would write them and he would publish them, the very division of labor I had in mind. *Mohawk* was only the beginning. A corner had been turned.

It was nearly midnight when our train pulled back into New Haven. Barbara had been reading mail she'd hurriedly stuffed in her purse that morning as we headed out the door, so she didn't immediately respond when I said I was starved and a pizza would really hit the spot. Wooster Street was just a few short blocks away and Frank Pepe's might still be open. "Look at this," she said, holding up the twenty-dollar bill that had slipped from one of the birthday cards.

Don't kid yourself. Nothing beats a white clam pizza at Frank Pepe's. Not surf. Not turf. If I had any idea how to make such a pizza, I'd give you the recipe.

# Beach Food

## Michelle Wildgen

STEVE AND THE LOBSTER AND I WERE STANDING, SWEATING, IN the little beach house kitchen in Delaware. On the counter the lobster arched its back and raised a knowing claw in our direction.

I thought we should kill it with a sharp knife slid into the back of the shell, where the head and sectioned carapace meet, then cut it up and cook it.

"I heard that's more humane," I said. I also thought, for some obscure reason, it might make the meat taste better. I should give this fresh lobster the most delicious death I could. Yet I hoped I might con Steve into being the killer. In the past I had persuaded him to cook and dismember a lobster for paella without any of the requisite tools. It turned out those tools were both well-designed and necessary. A hammer and pliers from the garage were just not the same.

At least here we had the claw crackers, the little silver picks. No respectable beach house, not even this tiny, out-dated, and slightly musty one, could do without them.

"There's no way I'm stabbing the lobster," Steve said. I lost my nerve, too, and opened the pot of steaming water.

It was the last night of our honeymoon and we were making seafood soup. (I'd done this back in Wisconsin but it was never what it should be with Midwestern seafood.) We boiled the lobster, cut apart the scarlet carapace, and kept it for stock. The rosy-speckled meat we cut into disks. I looked in vain for roe, hoping I could mash it with butter and swirl it into the soup at the end. We added more garlic, the lobster, the shrimp, the crab, the clams, and the tomatoes. At the end we threw in tarragon. We cooked together, Steve peeling the shrimp and slicing the garlic into sticky rounds. I chopped and skinned tomatoes and steamed the corn.

When we finally sat down, it was dark, the day losing its heat. We lit candles, opened fresh beers. For an appetizer I had poured the clams in a pot with garlic and shallot and butter, decanted a small river of wine, and steamed them open in it. We cooked so many we had to eat them from a mixing bowl.

But the soup—the soup was scarlet, flecked with green leaves and ivory lobster, the yellow ruffled edges of the clams peeking above the surface amid the shreds of crab. It tasted splendid: heavy on the garlic and the red chilies, the briny scent of the seafood, the browned crumb of the bread we'd toasted to go with it. It wasn't delicate, except for the texture of the fish. It's not a soup to get elegant with—no purées, no cream or tiny spoons. It was messy, heady, spicy, speckled with olive oil and herbs.

It was not a dish for someone with a newly diagnosed, un-predictable seafood allergy. A week earlier, I'd discovered—via swelling, itching, and a trip to the ER as my throat began to close—that I was one of those people. I was telling myself the culprit was only a specific type of cheap frozen crab Rangoon. So far on this trip I had eaten shellfish but no crab Rangoon, and nothing had happened. I hoped to continue my streak of luck with the soup, but I suspected the allergy was not as limited as I wanted it to be.

As we began to eat, Steve watched me for signs of a reaction. I was watching him, too. It was true I should have been more cautious with seafood, but neither should he have been drinking the beers we'd just cracked or the gin and tonics we'd sipped beforehand. I had just begun to suspect that as well.

For six years we never considered marriage. Then in 2000 we got engaged, married, and moved to the East Coast all in three months. In June, I had proposed and Steve had agreed. Then he got food poisoning. This happened two days after we got engaged, at a barbecue where we began the rounds of announcements and watched a friend poke raw chicken breast and undercooked bratwurst around a tepid grill. Really it was obvious that someone would be sick. I announced the engagement to my family by myself while Steve stayed home, moaning on the bathroom floor and croaking weak but affable thanks when my parents phoned him.

Then, in August, the day after we got married, that crab Rangoon swelled my throat slowly closed. We joked that these were omens. We could do that out of confidence, even hubris: we mocked the way our milestones were attended by vomiting and emergency rooms, and then forgot about it.

We also forgot to plan a honeymoon, but luckily someone we knew owned a little bungalow on the Delaware shore. It was a hairsbreadth from dilapidated and the wiring was going. We ate our meals on mismatched china at an old wood table on the back porch, which was lined with tough green indoor-outdoor carpeting. The last visitors had left a charred candle in a discolored bone holder, which we lit every evening. Our gin and tonics tasted of citronella, the scent of our sunscreen hovering over the glass.

Other people's kitchens tend to be a nightmare of dull knives, treacherous glass cutting boards, and hostile, diminutive saucepans. This one was in better shape: the knife was fairly dull but not a cheap serrated one, there was a wooden cutting board, and most importantly there were two deep mixing bowls and a huge stockpot. This was fortunate, because we intended nothing less than a shellfish extravaganza.

We regarded the ocean less as a place to swim than as a vast buffet. Our first night in town, smelling the salt and kelp in the air, we stopped at a bar and ordered blue crabs dredged in fiery reddish-orange seasoning, dumping a pile of them onto a newspaper-covered picnic table. It was my favorite kind of seafood: a meal you ate with your hands, till your fingers and mouth burned. We drank a pitcher of cold, pale beer from plastic cups. Steve was peaceful, happy. He didn't drink too much, and I was beginning to relax again. As we ate we planned the week's meals—all shellfish.

I made the pretense of caution, pausing as I started each meal to gauge any reactions. I was supposed to carry a couple of EpiPens, but kept forgetting. Who really carried medicine everywhere they went; who worried that way? I had never believed that all these things really applied to me. And we kept getting away with it: meal after meal I ate seafood without consequence, night after night Steve drank wine or beer like a normal person. Though Steve would stop me as we left the beach house to be sure I had my EpiPens and question whether we should order blue crab by the pound, I chose to see it as sweet, as someone trying out the new role of husband and worrier. I think I responded with shrugs, with exclamations over the sudden lightness of his hair. He is a true blond, for whom an hour in the sun gilds his eyebrows and lashes, bleaches out his thick hair straight to the roots. It makes him slightly unreal: his height and breadth, the flaxen hair and blue eyes. He is a peculiar and possibly brilliant dancer. He has never been in a fight in his life. He once stopped off for bigger pants on the way to dinner.

On soup day we drove around to various shops. The seafood store for lobster, clams, and shrimp. A farm stand for tarragon, tomatoes, garlic, and corn. A plain grocery store for olive oil, butter, and bread. At the liquor store we bought wine to cook with, lager to drink, and gin and limes for cocktails. It would never have occurred to us not to include alcohol in a great meal: I was always amazed and slightly appalled by people who could order iced tea with dinner. Though I tried to suppress it, I had even felt the same judgmental thrum when Steve's father, an alcoholic who had not had a drink in thirty years, ordered ice water at a French restaurant. We believed in too much rather than running out. Neither of us was ready to change that, any more than I would forego all shellfish until I absolutely had to.

That last night I gorged myself on the seafood soup so filled with shellfish it was barely even soup. I started with a chunk of lobster: if I were going to have to cut this short, I wouldn't have wasted my time on shrimp. I took the first bite, and Steve sat back and watched me. It was sort of a ritual: the slow chew, the thoughtful inventory of my responses. Was that sunburn or the first ominous, tentative itch of my skin? I was slightly flushed and warm, but it might have been the warmth on the porch. It might simply have been pleasure over the honeymoon, the meal. Did my lips feel numb at all, did my scalp or face tingle? Maybe; maybe—but the soup was peppery. The sensory recall of that one attack was fading already.

"Well?" Steve said. I ate a clam. It was a little on the chewy side, but I didn't mind.

"I think I'm fine," I said. "I really don't feel anything abnormal." Saying it made us both relax. We settled in and ate the soup, dipping our garlic bread into it and stirring it sensuously with our spoons to make it last.

"Maybe we should have gotten wine," Steve said. "The soup kind of deserves it."

"There's wine in the soup," I pointed out. "It's too spicy for most wines, anyway. Unless we'd found a nice dry rosé."

We were both quiet for a moment, disappointed we'd neglected the proper wine. I liked talking about what wine we should have, what drink went with which dish. I didn't want to have to give that up, either. I did not say this, but stirred my soup until I found a lobster claw, the perfect shape of the meat still mimicking its lost shell, and ate it all at once.

Nothing happened. The allergy would lie dormant, resting up, for another six months. I was certain I must have

dodged a bullet—it was all a mistake, surely. Every time I
lucked out it was pure relief, even delight, to be able to have
what I wanted, as much as I wanted.

We opened the extra beer because we didn't have to drive
and didn't care about hangovers. We lit more candles and
played strip poker. I talked about squeezing in one more
paper tablecloth full of blue crabs before we drove back to
New York the next day to start new jobs and new schools
and settle into a new apartment.

Later that winter, after months of eating shellfish like
anyone else, a meal at a tapas restaurant on First Avenue
proved the final straw for my dithering immune system,
which decided on *allergic* once and for all and landed me in
Beth Israel. As I lay in a bed hooked up to IVs and monitors,
I recalled the way I'd almost mistaken sunburn, the heat of a
few chilies, or a nervous flush for the first symptoms of
shock. It turned out there was no mistaking the real thing.
This time my hair had stood up on end. The tingling that
had ranged over my skin had been electric and distinct, almost crackling; my mouth had swelled and numbed so thoroughly that I felt my own face as meat, as not belonging to
me at all. In the hospital I finally understood the obvious,
that vacations full of seafood were an impossibility for me.

But at the beach that summer I hadn't yet believed in
such an insurmountable problem. We had been married for
two weeks.

Here is another event from that same summer: in July, still
back in Wisconsin before the wedding, Steve and I had
walked to a bar. We played pool with a guy we'd just met.
We all liked each other, and I remember feeling that all

was going well, that I was funny, Steve was funny, everyone was funny.

Somewhere along the way, the night changed. We were still playing pool with our new acquaintance, still sipping at beers, when I realized something about Steve was off. His voice had gotten louder, his jokes were duller, and then the worm turned entirely. I can't remember the exact moment when I knew, but I remember the guy looking down at the pool table and away from us, then quietly drifting to another part of the room. I don't remember what Steve had said, maybe some inappropriate joke, but I realized he was drunk. Not the pleasant, sensory-laden buzz of a few drinks after work or wine with every course at a pricey dinner, but sloppy, mortifyingly drunk. In all the years I'd known him, through years at a heavy-drinking Midwestern college and lots of bars and countless boozy dinners, I had very rarely seen him like this. Yet this was the second time in a matter of weeks that he'd been badly out of control. I wasn't sure how it had happened. I thought I knew what he'd been drinking, but maybe he'd been ordering shots when I wasn't looking. Much later he would tell me he'd begun every evening with a big head start. My first beer might be his seventh. The vodka bottle in our apartment, which I thought was the same one for months, was refilled again and again.

We had just become the embarrassing couple in the bar. Every bar has one, and everyone dreads their arrival. Walking home I was silent; Steve veered between sappy, seductive, and annoyed at the silence. He wove slightly into the grass and back onto the sidewalk again. At home he went to bed and passed out.

There was no reason he'd drunk so much, he later told

me. No secret grief, no special fear over the wedding. It just happened.

I knew that this was trouble, as surely as I knew the night I met him that I would see him again. I had watched for this. His father was a recovered alcoholic sober for many years; his grandfather an alcoholic who died of it. It ran through the men in his family the same way blue eyes did, or the shape of their noses, and deep down I knew what I was seeing. I asked myself if I was really going to do what, perhaps, I ought to: cancel the wedding, tell him to stay in Madison while I moved across the country. Was I going to dump someone after six years because he got drunk? This was both a gross oversimplification and also the basic truth.

There are so many things that can go wrong with those late summer meals if you don't time them right or if luck is simply not on your side. You can get impatient and try for tomatoes before they're ready, or end up with puckered, brunette ears of corn from a store that calls itself a farm stand but is really an outdoor A&P. The bread can be pallid. The clams can die in your fridge, sad tongues of flesh drooping over the lips of their shells. The lobster can be stringy, the crab frozen, the parsley dried.

The last meal of our honeymoon was perfect, it was true, but we missed the luck part of the equation. We thought it was our doing. The corn and tomatoes had come to us with skins stretched taut with juice, the shellfish as lively as is required by the rather brutal pleasures of eating seafood. It had nothing to do with us, but as we ate that late summer meal, we thought that this was the next thing, that we were on the verge and it would be splendid. We had changed almost everything in our lives, thrown our lot together. The surfeit of cash from the wedding gave us a taste of what a little wealth might feel like. The sea had washed our new rings so clean they sparkled. The filaments at the edges of Steve's lashes and eyebrows were bright gold.

You couldn't have guessed, looking at him as we sat on the porch and talked idly about the lemon-scented blueberry cobbler we would have for dessert, that he would turn into someone totally different, someone whose eyes went as dead as a trout's, who within a few years would stumble in without looking at me long after work, after midnight if at all. I could not have known he would someday come out of a blackout to find himself walking along a rural highway twenty miles north of our house, still carrying his briefcase, but I think he knew, even then, that something like that was on its way.

The cobbler that night was rich and still warm when we ate it, the syrupy blueberries staining the biscuit and the vanilla ice cream. Its texture was rustic (I had been experimenting with cornmeal), studded with bits of lemon peel that candied as they baked. We ate cobbler again for breakfast, and then we drove north.

Five years later, we live more like monks: our herbal tea after dinner, the endless seltzer. I don't touch shellfish, too frightened by the second, ferocious attack to risk it. For several months after the honeymoon I'd gone on eating as I pleased and never carrying the EpiPen, cooking feasts of lobster and shrimp and ordering blue crab and oysters with an appetite like a gangster. Then came the clams and shrimp and scallops and squid and sardines at the tapas bar, and the trip to

Beth Israel, and that was it for shellfish. There is no longer a special wine with an anniversary dinner or beer on a hot afternoon. There is not supposed to be anything alcoholic at all, Steve is supposed to be sober, but in truth it is a cycle. Weeks of sobriety, then the fall. Every month or so it returns, secreted in a briefcase, brought in from the trunk of the car when I'm not home. We're long past pretending these binges are accidental, or that even a single glass of wine is acceptable. So instead of too much wine at dinner, it's the bottle in the closet, the thermos tucked among the ceiling tiles. He can only hide it for a day or so. Then we clear the place out, dump the bottles, and the next attempt begins.

Monastic life, if only intermittent, has its benefits, the biggest one being that ninety percent of the time I have him back, the person I knew for the first six years. But sometimes I wake in the middle of the night, the bed next to me empty. Steve is home; but he's on the couch, and I go and stand over him, knowing that he falls asleep out there when he has hidden a bottle somewhere in the house and waited till I've gone to bed to get it. In these moments I don't know what will follow—whether I'll go to work or call a moving van. It could be thirty more years if he recovers, or it could be one more day.

Now it's summer again, and it comes back to me how entwined with heat are the pleasures of dry rosé and cocktails and beer. I think of that week at the beach fondly, bitterly, as if it were a lost paradise and not a beach like any other. The house was just a house, a free shelter near the sand. That dinner was glorious because we were being granted a respite before we even understood it. The sharp scent of the flickering candle, the lime on our fingers, the sea-sweet lobster,

the torn basil leaves, and the buttered clams frilled with yellow muscle—it was all a mirage, but we actually lived inside
it. Nothing existed beyond that little house and the dark,
starred beach with its water foaming whitely around our
feet, and nothing malevolent came inside its boundaries.
We had inklings of what was coming, what circled us even
then. But during that week, that last night, those clues had
all receded, or else we simply pushed them back. The future
waited, as it always does, melting patiently into the hazy
edge of the horizon.

## Clams with Garlic and Wine

A big slosh of olive oil, plus more for brushing the bread

2 to 3 shallots, coarsely chopped

6 garlic cloves, coarsely chopped, plus 2 halved garlic cloves

2 pounds clams, scrubbed clean and soaked in water with
   cornmeal or salt, whichever you prefer

A cup or two of dry white wine

Salt and pepper

A handful of chopped parsley

4 thick slices sourdough or other hearty bread

SERVES 2 TO 3: In a saucepan deep enough to fit all the clams,
heat the slosh of olive oil over medium heat, and add the shallots
and chopped garlic. Cook till they are golden. Put in the clams
and pour the wine over, adding more if it doesn't look generously
steamy enough. Cover the pan tightly.

   While the clams are cooking, toast the slices of sourdough or
other bread. Rub them with a cut clove of garlic and brush with
olive oil, then sprinkle with salt.

   After a few minutes, peer into the saucepan. When the clams
are all open, divide them between two bowls and pour the broth

over them. Scatter the parsley over before serving. Serve with
the bread. Add salt and pepper as needed.

## Seafood Soup

**SOME COMBINATION OF THE FOLLOWING, WHATEVER YOU LIKE**

1 lobster

Olive oil

A few dried red chili peppers, to taste

Many cloves of garlic—at least 5

A small onion, chopped

Lots of dry white wine

A few pounds of beautiful late-summer tomatoes, skinned
  and chopped (fresh is ideal, but high-quality canned will
  be better than out-of-season tomatoes)

Salt and pepper

12 clams or mussels

12 shrimp, ideally with shell and head on, but why quibble?

½ pound crabmeat, picked over for cartilage

Fish, such as red snapper, monkfish, or any white-fleshed fish

Fresh tarragon, basil, or parsley

**SERVES 6 TO 8:** Steam or boil the lobster for a little less time than
you normally would. Let it cool in the fridge a bit, then remove
the meat from the shell and save the shell, the green tomalley,
and any roe. Cut the meat into bite-size pieces.

Heat a few tablespoons of olive oil over medium heat in a big,
deep, heavy pan. Add the chilies, garlic, and onion and cook until
the garlic and onion are pale gold. Add the lobster shell and try
to smash it slightly with a spoon without accidentally flipping it
out of the pan. Add lots of wine. Let this combination simmer
gently for ten minutes or so before removing the lobster shell.
Then add the tomatoes and salt to taste and simmer a little

longer. Begin adding the seafood and fish in order of cooking time: the clams or mussels, the shrimp, the crabmeat, the fish, and finally the lobster just to heat it through. If you require more stock at any point, just add more wine and some water, and be sure to simmer the alcohol away. Taste toward the end for salt and pepper, and drizzle with olive oil if you like. Garnish with lots of torn tarragon or basil leaves.

You could also add fennel, sliced and cooked like onion, and a pinch of saffron, and finish it off with orange juice. All of these things are delicious. I have added fresh summer corn at times as well, which makes it more chowdery and hearty, a little sweeter. This dish is best served with toasted bread to dip into the broth.

## Lazy Blueberry Cobbler

A true cobbler has biscuit dough rolled out over the top of the fruit. I don't know that I have ever had a true cobbler; I grew up eyeing this shortcut version of my mother's as it cooled on the back of the stove. There was a brief ambitious period in my early twenties when I might have tried out a real cobbler, but I have since given in to my own laziness.

4 tablespoons (½ stick) unsalted butter

2 cups blueberries (I often try to pack in more, reasoning that it offsets the butter)

1 cup flour (or ½ cup flour and ½ cup fine cornmeal)

1 cup sugar

1 teaspoon baking powder

1 cup milk

1 tablespoon pure vanilla extract

Zest of 1 lemon

**SERVES 5 TO 6:** Heat the oven to 350 degrees. Melt the butter in the glass or ceramic dish in which you'll bake the cobbler. Add the blueberries. In a bowl, combine the flour, sugar, and baking powder. Add the milk and vanilla and mix till smooth. Pour on top of the fruit. Do not stir the fruit into the batter. Bake until just brown, 35 to 40 minutes. Serve warm with vanilla ice cream.

This turns into hot fruit with a golden-brown cakey top that seems so moist it's almost custardy. Other fruit works just as well—pitted sour cherries or peaches especially. I have also made this with as little as two tablespoons of butter, so that I could think of it as "breakfast cobbler."

# By the River Cousin

## Claire Messud

IN MY MIND, AT LEAST, THE INN IN THE VALLEY, BY THE LITTLE
river Cousin, a few kilometers from Avallon, near Chablis, is
the place to which Camus and the Gallimards were headed
on the day of their fatal car crash. I'm not sure why I insist,
against reason, upon this belief: they were returning to Paris;
it was wintertime—surely not the season for a supper *en
plein air*; and the restaurant, while fine, does not perhaps
merit a wide detour. But in the twelve—or is it fourteen?—
years since we made our way along the winding, sun-dappled
road, following the curves of the water, to the former mill,
I have stubbornly maintained—to others, as well as to
myself—what surely is a falsehood.

It was my father's birthday. In memory, it was my father's
sixtieth birthday; but this, again, must be wrong. That
would have made the date June 29, 1991; but I remember

distinctly—and of this I am certain—that James and I shared a room, which we would never, in the company of my parents, have done before we were married. We were married in June 1992; so in fact, it must have been 1993. It has to have been. A birthday, nevertheless, but a less significant birthday. When a gathering seems so perfect—not just as it is remembered, but as it is lived—it is impossible not to want to infuse it with moment. In truth, it was just an inn. Just a river. Just a birthday.

James and I lived in London, then. We were driving down to my grandparents' place in Toulon, for a family holiday by the sea. We drove an ancient Saab, of a dull sky blue, with low, wide mud guards that lent the car a bell-bottomed aspect, perfectly in keeping with its age. If there were people in the back seat, the low-slung car would scrape the asphalt when turning a corner. Thrice stolen from the streets of London, thrice returned (albeit once without the cassette tape of Gertrude Stein reading her poetry; which precious item had been replaced by rap music. We think the thieves took Gertrude for a rapper), it was a trusty and reliable old banger. It carried us through France at its stately pace without once threatening failure, even on the steepest inclines.

The entire trip lives vividly in my mind's eye, each night a surprise. On the way down we stopped in a dusty old hotel with sagging mattresses in the forgotten center of Laon; at the converted mill near Avallon; at a trim new auberge with a swimming pool, surrounded by farms, on an island in the river outside Avignon where, when we walked toward the fields after supper, the sky was so black about us that it was as if we stepped into the void. On the way back north, we traveled to the west: the first night found us in a small medieval castle a few miles from Carcassonne, dining beneath vaulted stone, with slit windows in the battlements overlooking a precipitous and verdant ravine; the second—and this, too, proved an extraordinary evening—in a village inn by a lake in the mountains near Vichy, a place untouched by time, where we perched in the small dining room on ladder-back cane chairs, surrounded by silent locals, small men in flat caps and their thick-armed wives in tight nylon dresses, eating pâté, grilled fish, crème caramel, all of it fresh, simple, flavorful, perfect, and all there was on offer, for a grand total of thirty-five francs—about six dollars—per person, including wine, and then retired to our room with its mounded duvet and four-poster bed, to watch, upon its ancient television, mysteriously, as if sent by God, a segment of Claude Lanzmann's *Shoah*. We have always referred to this as our "Vichy France Experience." On the third night, in a fit of extravagance, we paid ourselves a stay just south of Paris, in a grand manor house set in splendid gardens that had belonged to the éminence grise—a cardinal, but not Richelieu—of one of the French monarchs. Our room was small, but its ceilings were vastly high, and the full-length windows, draped in navy blue, opened onto a balustraded balcony overlooking a grand emerald stretch of lawn. There, as in Avallon and Avignon, we dined outside, in the hot, still, late dusk, in the smell of summer grass and hedges, watching the midges swarm around the marble statuary. At that last stopover, it was breakfast that delighted us: the heavy silver cutlery, the burnished coffee pot, the steaming jug of milk, the fresh-squeezed orange juice, the croissants and jam.

"This," I told my husband, "is what I remember from my childhood. This is the hotel breakfast of my childhood."

And the taste of it—with great Proustian force—brought back the mornings when we would arrive in Paris, from Australia, where we lived when I was small, or from some intermediary point: thickly gray, damp dawns, when we would check into our hotel—for years the Windsor, near the Champs-Élysées, because it belonged to the company for which my father worked; and then, after they sold it, never again the Windsor—and make our way to a café on the still-deserted Champs, where we were the only patrons beneath the heat lamps, on the wet pavement, because it was so very early, so early that even the cars, swishing down the slick avenue with their headlights still on, were rare, and where we watched Paris, little by little, and then in a great rush, awaken. The Windsor, in the early days, was as it had been for almost a century, with its ornate oriental rugs and velvet armchairs, its dark wood and low sconces, its metal-caged elevator—I remember the sound and shiver of its unfurling metal gate; and the natty uniform of its operator—and the grand piano in the lobby, played, each evening, by an old lady who lived, in permanence, upstairs, and who was forever conflated, in my mind, with the Old Lady out of *Babar*.

But I digress: the meal, the extraordinary meal. We assembled for it. It was the purpose of our gathering, the purpose of having chosen that hotel over any other—the *Michelin* recommended it, in the area, particularly for its restaurant; and I had booked it from London, sight unseen—and we had all come a certain distance. James and I had driven that day from Laon. My parents had flown from New York, my sister from Toronto, to Paris, where they had met at Roissy, had rented a car, and made their way to Avallon.

Arriving in the late afternoon, as the sun speckled the

gravel drive and, beyond the bristling hedge, a patio and sloping riverbank through the overhanging trees, we were shown through the hotel's simple lobby and up to our rooms. Ours, spacious and spare, faced the river, and that was its chief advantage. There were two narrow beds, a dresser, a hard chair. We were not displeased to find our accommodations of a near monastic simplicity: there was nothing pretentious about Le Moulin des Ruats, but instead there was an almost religious devotion to its food. If you have eaten well, the atmosphere seemed to suggest, in beautiful surroundings, then what does it matter that the walls of your room are bare, its lamps few and dim? The sheets were clean and stiffly starched, the bathrooms serviceable, spotless; everything was, as the French say, *correcte*. Somehow, this seemed in itself a perfection. We wouldn't have wanted more.

It was the first time our family had met like this—like adults!—in an unknown French village, in the waning day, all of us united after long travel. It had been my suggestion, my doing, and there's no doubt that I felt proud that it proved a success. But it also felt like a beginning, like life as it would be lived. It seemed that there would be, henceforth, many such times: family gatherings, peaceable (in a family rarely peaceable), in beautiful, unimagined places. Annually, perhaps. In this way, the world's endless variety would open to us, season by season, room by room, meal by meal. It would be something we would get better at. It was unlike us, but it would become like us. We would stop being a quarrelsome, ornery, existentially anxious bunch, would transform, instead, into a family of light touches, tinkling laughter, effortless happiness. Our lives would resemble a Jean Renoir film, or a Manet painting. This, I believed, with a passion for which I now feel wistful forgiveness, was what being an adult would be like.

I have to confess that I have no idea what we ate. I remember that I savored every mouthful, that each bite was an explosion of flavors in my mouth. I wrote in my diary what I, at least, had eaten. I came across the record a few years ago, and in re-reading, relived the experience, could taste again the savory, the sour, the sweet. But I've lost that *aide-mémoire*, stored irretrievably in some unmarked box, moved from house to house, perhaps discarded, and without it, I cannot name the dishes. I don't know what it says about me that I've forgotten my most memorable meal. But things are never about what they're about. Of course.

I can tell you—because the hotel and restaurant, now, in the Internet age, have a virtual presence, a website in which everything is presented in miniature, and the magic, the inimitability of it, is vanished—what their specialties are. The river trout *en bleu*, for example; or the mille-feuille of turnips and tomato confit in a honey and coriander vinaigrette; the *croustade*, a regional brioche-like cake, for dessert. I can tell you that they offer smoked trout and fresh salmon in aspic, served on a warm potato salad; or rabbit preserved in garlic and garnished with black olives; or filet mignon of pork with a Roquefort sabayon. But even as I imagine them—relatively simple, traditional dishes, exquisitely prepared—I can't be certain that all those years ago any of these was on the menu. I can't tell you if I ate one of these, or something else entirely. I can tell you that my father hesitated, was about to order a petit Chablis, and then decided, in a moment of festive extravagance and at the waiter's subtle urging, to opt for a far better wine. I remember the wine, cold and crisp. It was delicious. I remember my fingers upon the wineglass, and its summer sweat.

We ate at a table beneath an old and spreading tree at the river's edge. The cloth was pristine, the crystal sparkling, but the birds twittered over our heads and the burble of the water ran constant at our backs. As we ate, the night slowly fell around us, and our features were melted, simplified, in the flickering candlelight: we became kinder, easier, more benevolent. Delighted by the novelty and grace of it all, we simply, unselfconsciously enjoyed ourselves together. The river, in the dark, sounded louder, our voices softer, more mellifluous. The evening air had not a hint of chill, nor was it too warm. It did not blow, but breathed, like an intimate. It was as you would wish a summer evening air.

We met at the inn. We ate our supper beneath the trees, by the river. We drank the fine Chablis, in the growing dark. We conversed, my husband, my sister, my parents, and I. We laughed. We all felt the magic of it. We spoke of feeling the magic of it. We felt that it mattered. It seemed we had never, together, known such a time.

In the morning, we parted. My sister came with James and me, and our parents set off on their own. We would find them again in Toulon, two days later. The three of us drove first to Vézelay, to the glorious cathedral upon its melancholy, fateful rise above the plain. It was summer, then, and the cobbles clattered with tourists, their buses lined up three deep. The pilgrims called to each other in a Babel of languages: they, like we, came from far away and everywhere. The relics of Mary Magdalene, unlike Le Moulin des Ruats, merit as great a detour as necessary. The square outside the church was lined with shops peddling Catholic kitsch—

fluttering ribbons, candles, statues, portraits of Jesus and his bleeding heart—and we did not loiter. Years later, James and I would return, in winter, to find the square before the church abandoned, and ourselves silent observers as a clutch of hessian-clad nuns and monks slipped silently across the stones, in sandals in the snow. As we wandered the chill corners of the cathedral, gaped up at its arches, stepped down into its silent crypt, we were suddenly visited by the sound of singing, an extraordinary, pure music, like water. And when we followed it, we found the nuns and monks upon their knees in a quiet side chapel, beatific, singing their prayers. It remains the closest I have ever come to seeing God; and it made me want very much to believe.

But on that first summer morning, Vézelay was a disappointment, a bustling rabble of grasping believers, all of them hoping for the experience we would later have, or for some representation of that experience (a glow-in-the-dark Mary statuette? A key-chain with a dangling Saint Francis?). It rather spoiled our otherworldly sense of the previous evening, and we did not tarry long before driving off, and south, in our dignified but aged Saab, toward the dusty heat of Avignon, and the sea beyond.

I think even then I held in my mind that Avallon, and, by extension, Le Moulin des Ruats, was Camus's final destination, the place toward which he and his friends sped on his last afternoon, sated by a hearty lunch and doubtless a glass too many of red wine. This certainty, surely false, may have been born of many things: of my desire, however tangentially, to commune with greatness; of my fantasies about France, which is my father's homeland and, in a lesser and partial and perhaps imaginary way, my own; of my particular adoration, at that time in my life, for the figure of Camus, a *pied-noir* like my own family, who committed his life in an ultimately confused and all-too-human way to justice, truth, and literature all at once. It doesn't ultimately matter whether Camus even knew of the existence of the place—after all, he might have done. But the wish for it— a strange one for me, who am usually so profoundly and tediously wedded to the truth—persists, after all these years. That evening, my family shared in that place a perfect illusion, an illusion of perfection, and a reminder of the need for illusion itself.

Here is why it remains with me: because it was beautiful, and simple, and the food delicious, and the weather perfect. Because we were together, as adults, as a family, for the first time. Because we did not quarrel; indeed, we appreciated each other as much as we did the food, the wine, the familial river Cousin. Because I thought—I believed!—that it was a beginning, that there would be many such times, too many to count, that this was an example of what we waited for, why it was worth forsaking the joys of childhood, and growing up. Each moment a surprise, and a surprise without flaw. It remains with me because, although I've had many wonderful meals, and lovely gatherings, no such evening has come to me since; and because I've learned that even the simplest of pleasures are rare and precious. Perhaps these most of all.

# My Dinner with Andy Warhol's Friends

## Michael Stern

THE ONE MEAL I FEAR I SHALL NEVER FORGET WAS IN A RESTAURANT. Its telltale moment came at the very beginning when glasses of water arrived. We were a table of four at New Jersey's old Clam Broth House, the place Jane and I had chosen as the right location to host a welcome-to-the-USA dinner for Thomas Ammann, Switzerland's leading art dealer, and his good friend Mathias. The waiter managed to carry four full tumblers in one hand so that his fingers, sunk deep in each below the waterline, looked like brined sausage links and his thumb functioned to align the quartet as he set them all in the center of the table. In his other hand was a basket piled high with packets of saltine crackers, some of which bounced out onto the table when he plopped it down. He used the front of his shirt to wipe our drinking water off his meaty mitt, then reached into his ass pocket for an order pad. "What'll it be?" said he.

And so began the night of a thousand embarrassments. Actually, it began well before dinner, when we drove from our house in Connecticut into New York to pick up our Swiss guests at the townhouse where they were staying on the Upper East Side. But before I share the gruesome details—before, during, and after the meal from hell—I need to explain how we wound up in a loutish fish house in Hoboken trying to show two European sophisticates a good time in America.

The year before, 1971, Jane and I had spent a week in Switzerland so I could interview the expatriate Hollywood director Douglas Sirk, subject of my thesis in film history at Columbia University. Douglas and his wife, Hilde, had made their home down in the lake city of Lugano, but knowing that this was our first trip abroad and being a gentlemanly fellow, he had advised us beforehand that when we arrived we would be met in Zurich by two young friends of his, Mathias and Thomas. He assured us they would be wonderful companions for our first evening in one of the great cities of Europe.

Travel novices, we were in the throes of a dizzying fog of jet lag when the phone in our Zurich hotel room rang and woke us from fitful naps. It was dinnertime. Mathias and Thomas were downstairs. We shook their hands as they welcomed us speaking surprisingly good English. They had a large car and uniformed driver waiting in the street to take us all to dinner, but in our confusion and naiveté, the ride's class was lost on us. We perceived the two of them as fresh-faced boys from the Swiss mountains—happy yokels who, in the spirit of so many admirable guys in Douglas Sirk's melodramas, represented the goodness of nature and of a simple life spent yodeling in fresh air.

At the restaurant they chose, we ate delicious veal sausage and *rösti* potatoes and a roast beef dish called Robespierre served from a rolling silver cart. We drank some wicked cocktails called Ladykillers and fine wines of our hosts' choosing, all of it served by a staff of deft professionals who made every moment of the meal unfold effortlessly and with pleasure. In our warped vision the setting registered as some sort of quaint neighborhood tavern. We did make vague mental notes of the original paintings by Matisse, Kandinsky, Picasso, Matisse, and Chagall on the wall, but it was only after we returned to America that we realized the place they had taken us to was the Kronenhalle, one of the grand restaurants on the continent and certainly an echt-Swiss eating experience. How charming, we thought, that the country boys had taken the trouble to take us Americans to a place that was an important culinary landmark.

It was Carnival time in Zurich, and as we strolled the streets with our hosts after dinner, the masks and costumes on pedestrians amplified the surreal disconnection between what was all around us and how we were perceiving it. At one point in our perambulations, Mathias and Thomas took us down a street of beautiful old stone houses where the costumes on people standing in doorways and under street lamps were especially flamboyant, and especially feminine. "Drag queen prostitutes," the boys told us, "high end," translating the number of francs they charged into outrageous dollar amounts. But at this point in the evening, we were so blotto that even thousand-dollar hookers impressed us only in a vague, dreamy way. We woke up the next morning asking each other if the night before had really happened, then headed south and put it behind us. After two weeks in Lugano, we returned home to the U.S. with heads full of Douglas Sirk and his life in Hollywood. The night in Zurich stuck in our minds, but its ill-perceived details were indistinct remnants of memory, like scenes from a hashish hallucination.

A year later, we had a welcome opportunity to express gratitude to Douglas and Hilde for all their hospitality. They wrote us a letter saying that their friends Mathias and Thomas would be coming to New York, and asking would we like to see them for dinner? You bet we would, and just as Douglas had done when we had traveled to Switzerland, we would take care of everything. Leave the Swiss mountain boys in our hands and we would show them a good time.

Jane and I hadn't yet written the first edition of *Roadfood,* but the value of finding eateries that expressed local character was even then a guiding principle of our culinary adventuring. Thinking back on the Kronenhalle, we wished we had been more alert to all the aspects of its menu and personality that made it so perfectly Swiss. We were intent on finding its American equivalent, but New York baffled us. At the time, we were not alone in our belief that all the best restaurants in the city were French, and a French feast, no matter how fine, did not satisfy our intention to find a venue and a meal that these lads would remember forever as a unique American eating experience.

We made a campaign of choosing just the right place, rejecting all sorts of excellent eateries for all sorts of stupid reasons. Lower East Side delicatessens, Brooklyn pizzerias, and Midtown steak houses were all very New Yorky, but obvious and not important enough. Grand Central's Oyster Bar or Tavern on the Green? Too touristy. The Four Seasons? Too expense-accounty. Then a friend, whose name I have mercifully forgotten, suggested the Clam Broth House in Hoboken. We had never been there ourselves. All we knew about this place was its famous signs outside: two huge neon-rimmed hands, each of which had a fat finger pointing downward. Hoboken sounded way cool, what with it being Frank Sinatra's home town, not to mention home of the Tootsie Roll; and the very idea of going to New Jersey for dinner had a certain reverse-chic cachet that appealed to our oh-so-refined sensibilities. The Clam Broth House, this "friend" explained, was an 1899-vintage neighborhood tavern specializing in excellent seafood and patronized by the uppermost echelon of New Jersey wiseguys. The movie *On the Waterfront*, about crime and corruption in the old shipyards, had been filmed in Hoboken. Excellent! Driving to New Jersey to eat lobster with mobsters would make this excursion into an eating adventure that no one other than we clever Sterns could orchestrate. It would be an evening Mathias and Thomas would never forget.

Oh, how true that turned out to be. To pick them up, we arrived at the address they had given us in Manhattan, which they had described as the home of a friend who was putting them up during their visit. We were the proud drivers of a nearly new Super Beetle, which had a few more inches of space in the cabin than in a common Volkswagen bug. We rang the bell.

A wide-eyed Andy Warhol opened the door and nodded back to his houseguests to let them know we had arrived. The fact that the friend with whom they were staying was one of the world's best-known artists and a fixture of the New York social scene barely registered in our minds at that moment. We were on a mission; our course was fixed; reality could not intrude. The boys said good-bye to Andy and did a half-halt when they saw the double-parked VW. "We can drive," Thomas suggested. "Diana said we were free to use her car."

No, no, that wouldn't do. It was our party. We were in the driver's seat this night, so we shoehorned them into the back seat of the bug and headed for New Jersey. They explained to us that they were staying with Andy because Thomas was Andy's art dealer. Our picture of these two guys as log cabin–dwelling, lederhosen-wearing country bumpkins was evaporating quickly. Then, as we saw the light at the end of the Lincoln Tunnel, the Super Beetle coughed, sputtered, and died. Fortunately, the old-style Volkswagen was flimsy enough that Thomas, Mathias, and I easily were able to lean into the back bumper and push it out of the tunnel as Jane steered and passing drivers honked and yelled at us for tying up traffic. In the New Jersey daylight, I coaxed the boys back into the rear seat and, with Jane at the wheel, gave a mighty sustained thrust from the passenger's side door so that she could get the engine cranking. I heard Mathias whisper to Thomas, "We should have taken Diana's Corniche."

Jane tapped me on the knee. I looked at her. She was silently mouthing the word *Diana*, then gaping with a round mouth and wide eyes that I mistook for her imitation of a frightened fish. In fact, she was mouthing the word *Vogue*. The Diana of whom they spoke was Diana Vreeland, editor of *Vogue*, who was known for getting around town in a convertible Rolls-Royce Corniche.

Unphased, we putted off toward Hoboken in the Super Beetle. The Clam Broth House was a bleak façade in a dreary neighborhood that used to be an active dock and shipyard but had become an empty industrial wasteland, in no way colorful or picturesque. Its cheesy wood paneling sported droopy fishnets for decor; tables were bare and worn; and to call the staff brusque would be a kindness. The Kronenhalle this was not. Still, we soldiered on, hoping against hope that excellent food would transcend the ignominy of everything around us. I insisted that everybody get giant-size lobsters because that is what our tipster said was good to eat. Alas, this night whole steamed lobsters were unavailable. The waiter insisted that the kitchen's baked stuffed ones were even better, so that is what we got.

When the lobsters arrived is when Mathias and Thomas started talking German to each other. The creatures' desiccated meat was shrunken in their shells; the stuffing loaded into each carapace was sodden. On the side were piles of limp French fries and runny heaps of sugar-sweet coleslaw. Nobody did more than pick and push things around on the plate. Speaking English again, the boys mentioned that these lobsters were a lot different from the ones they had eaten the week before on the beach of a Greek Island where a fisherman they met had brought his catch still wriggling to the bonfire, and they ate under Mediterranean moonlight.

"Maine lobsters . . . big claws," I mumbled, knowing full well that the difference in lobster species did not explain the sorry ones laid before us that night. Jane, ever the cheerful host, tried valiantly to put the meal behind us by suggesting we drive back to New York for dessert.

We had parked on a slightly downhill Hoboken street, so it was easy for me to push-start the car to get us on our way to the other side of the river.

"What clubs are hot?" asked Thomas.

"Where's the scene?" Mathias wanted to know.

Jane's intention when she suggested going back to New York was to stop for an ice cream sundae at Rumpelmeyer's or drive out to Brooklyn for cheesecake at Junior's. Clubbing was not on the agenda. Clubbing is not what Jane and Michael Stern do, or ever have done. Still, we felt like complete boobs not knowing even the name of a happening place (forget about trying to get in the door). As we fumbled with the idea, mentioning the names of a few clubs that we had read about three years earlier (but having no idea where they were or if they still existed), the boys once more started talking German to each other in the back seat.

At this moment, we missed the chance to cut our losses. The sane thing to do would have been to drive back to Andy Warhol's place, drop them off so Andy could take them to the most happening place in town, and skulk away, only seventy-five-percent mortified with embarrassment. But no, we refused to admit defeat. On this night, we were going for one hundred ten percent. I had a brilliant idea: Times Square! This was long before Disney and its ilk moved in. Times Square was a cultural cesspool of porno theaters, cheap bars, and every kind of vice you could imagine. Since we knew no exciting club to visit, and since I vaguely recalled them taking us to see Zurich's hooker elite, I thought Times Square might just make up for all the evening's missteps. The previous year, Jane and I had made a television documentary about the shabby ex-crossroads of the world, and during the filming we had met a woman named Skippy the Grandma Stripper, who did an act with a monkey.

"Skippy, these are Mathias and Thomas. They are visiting from Switzerland," we said backstage at the club. In this case, "club" was hardly a cutting-edge venue filled with glitterati about to appear on Page 6 the next morning. It was a smoky strip-tease joint with a clientele of sad single men swilling watered-down whiskey and beer while they watched the performers take their clothes off to recordings of old Vaudeville drum-thumpers.

"Hello, boys," Skippy slurred in a sort of drunken Mae West voice. "Looking for a little fun?" She licked her lips, swirled her sheer dressing gown, and stepped toward them as if she was about to provide said fun. They jumped back as if approached by a leper. It was then that Frankie the monkey leapt up from the infant's crib where he had been snoozing and affixed himself to Thomas's face. Skippy managed to pull him off, at which point our two guests were suddenly gone from the dressing room. We bade a quick farewell to Skippy and followed them out through the grind house, where another stripper was spinning her pasties onstage, and onto Forty-Second Street. Was it my imagination, or were they quite literally running away from us?

No matter, we caught up with them and managed to convince them to get back in the car because, in fact, the street was crawling with all sorts of scary people. Happily, the car was now starting on its own, and as we drove east, they refused to speak any more English. It was at this time the full embarrassment of the evening began to wash over us. We did not want to imagine what these two guys would be telling Andy and Diana and all their friends in New York and Zurich about the two nincompoops from Connecticut whose idea of a good time was to cram into a dysfunctional VW, drive for mealy lobster dinners at a dump in New Jersey, then visit an aging stripper with a mean monkey.

We decided that rather than suffer such humiliation, it would be better to kill them. Earlier in the evening they had asked if we knew where to score any good dope. Our knowledge of dope dealers was about as deep as our knowledge of after-hours clubs, but on the way from Times Square, Jane piped up with the brilliant idea of taking them to Bryant Park. "It's a great place to score," she said, knowing that in fact it was a dope-dealer's haven and somehow forgetting the part about it also being an incredibly dangerous place for two foreign visitors to be wandering around in the middle of the night. I stopped the car across the street from the library at Bryant Park and got out so Mathias and Thomas could exit the backseat. I pointed into the darkness and told them they could score there. They trotted away from us and vanished. I got in the car and we drove home. Over the next few days, the newspapers carried no stories about two Swiss men found murdered in Byrant Park. Somehow, they survived.

Subsequently, we did often read accounts about Mathias and Thomas in the gossip columns that reported what New York's and Europe's art-world elite were up to. We remained on the mailing list of Thomas's Zurich gallery and every December received a fancy Christmas card. Several years after our dinner in Hoboken, Jane had the nerve to write to him and offer a long-overdue apology for everything that had happened that night. She suggested that the next time they came to New York, we should all go out to a really good meal. We never heard from them again.

# How I Learned to Eat

## Peter Mayle

THE EARLY PART OF MY LIFE WAS SPENT IN THE GASTRONOMIC wilderness of postwar England, when delicacies of the table were in extremely short supply. I suppose I must have possessed taste buds in my youth, but they were left undisturbed. Food was fuel, and in many cases not very appetizing fuel. I still have vivid memories of boarding school cuisine, which seemed to have been carefully color-coordinated: gray meat, gray potatoes, gray vegetables, gray flavor. At the time, I thought it was perfectly normal.

I was in for a pleasant shock. Not long after I became the lowliest trainee in an enormous multinational corporation, I was instructed to accompany my first boss, Mr. Jenkins, on a trip to Paris as his junior appendage. This was the way, so I was told, to start learning the ropes of big business. I should count myself lucky to have such an opportunity at the tender age of nineteen.

Jenkins was English and proud of it, English to the point of caricature, a role I think he took some pleasure in cultivating. When going abroad, he announced his nationality and armed himself against the elements with a bowler hat and a strictly furled umbrella. On this occasion, I was his personal bearer, and I had been given the important task of carrying his briefcase.

Before we left for the great unknown on the other side of the English Channel, Jenkins had been kind enough to give me some tips on dealing with the natives. One piece of advice was a model of clarity: I should never attempt to get involved with what he referred to as "their lingo." Speak English forcefully enough, he said, and they will eventually understand you. When in doubt, shout. It was a simple formula that Jenkins claimed had worked in outposts of the British Empire for hundreds of years, and he saw no reason for changing it now.

Like many of his generation, he had very little good to say about the French—an odd lot who couldn't even understand cricket. But he did admit that they knew their way around a kitchen, and one day he was graciously pleased to accept an invitation from two of his Parisian colleagues to have lunch; or, as Jenkins said, a spot of grub. It was the first memorable meal of my life.

We were taken to a suitably English address, the avenue Georges V, where there was (and still is) a restaurant called Marius et Janette. Even before sitting down, I could tell I was in a serious establishment, unlike anywhere I'd been before. It smelled different: exotic and tantalizing. There was the scent of the sea as we passed the display of oysters on their bed of crushed ice, the rich whiff of butter warming in a pan, and, coming through the air every time the kitchen door swung open, the pervasive—and to my untraveled nose, infinitely foreign—hum of garlic.

Jenkins surrendered his hat and umbrella as we sat down, and I looked with bewilderment at the crystal forest of glasses and the armory of knives and forks laid out in front of me. The trick was to start on the outside and work inward, I was told. But the correct choice of cutlery was a minor problem compared to making sense of the elaborate mysteries described on the pages of the menu. What was a *bar grillé?* What was a *loup à l'écaille?* And what in heaven's name was *aïoli?* All I had to help me was schoolboy French, and I hadn't been a particularly gifted schoolboy. I dithered over these puzzling choices in a fog of almost complete ignorance, too timid to ask for help.

Jenkins, quite unconsciously, came to my rescue. "Personally," he said, "I never eat anything I can't pronounce." He closed his menu with a decisive snap. "Fish and chips for me. They do a very decent fish and chips in France. Not quite like ours, of course."

With a sense of relief, I said I'd have the same. Our two French colleagues raised four surprised eyebrows. No oysters to start with? No *soupe de poisons?* The company was paying; there was no need to hold back. But Jenkins was adamant. He couldn't abide the texture of oysters—"slippery little blighters" was how he described them—and he didn't care for the way soup had a tendency to cling to his mustache. Fish and chips would suit him very nicely, thank you.

By this time, I was already enjoying a minor revelation,

which was the bread. It was light and crusty and slightly chewy, and I spread onto it some of the pale, almost white butter from the slab on a saucer in front of me. A slab. English butter in those days was highly salted and a lurid shade of yellow, and it was doled out in small, grudging pats. At the first mouthful of French bread and French butter, my taste buds, dormant until then, went into spasm.

The fish, a majestic creature that I think was sea bass, was ceremoniously presented, filleted in seconds with a spoon and fork, and arranged with great care on my plate. My previous experience of fish had been limited to either cod or plaice, heavily disguised, in accordance with the English preference, under a thick shroud of batter. In contrast, the sea bass, white and fragrant with what I now know was fennel, looked curiously naked. It was all very strange.

Even the chips, the *pommes frites*, didn't resemble the sturdy English variety. These chips, a golden pyramid of them served on a separate dish, were pencil-slim, crisp between the teeth, tender to chew, a perfect foil for the delicate flesh of the fish. It was lucky for me that I wasn't required to contribute to the conversation of my elders and betters; I was too busy discovering real food.

Then there was cheese. Or rather, there were a dozen or more cheeses, another source of confusion after years of having only the simple choice of Cheddar or Gorgonzola. I thought I recognized a vaguely familiar shape, safe and Cheddar-like, and pointed to it. The waiter insisted on giving me two other cheeses as well, so that I could compare the textural delights of hard, medium, and creamy. More of that bread. More signals of joy from the taste buds, which were making up for lost time.

*Tarte aux pommes.* Even I knew what that was; even Jenkins knew. "Excellent," he said. "Apple pie. I wonder if they have any proper cream." Unlike the apple pies of my youth, with a thick crust top and bottom, the tart on my plate was topless, displaying the fruit—wafers of apple, beautifully arranged in overlapping layers, glistening with glaze on a sliver of buttery pastry.

Too young to be offered an expense-account cigar and a balloon of brandy, I sat in a daze of repletion while my companions puffed away and considered a return to the cares of the office. I was slightly tipsy after my two permitted glasses of wine, and I completely forgot that I was responsible for the all-important Jenkins briefcase. When we left the restaurant I left it under the table, which demonstrated to him that I was not executive material, and which marked the beginning of the end of my career in that particular company. But, much more important, lunch had been a personal turning point, the loss of my gastronomic virginity.

It wasn't only because of what I had eaten, although that had been incomparably better than anything I'd eaten before. It was the total experience: the elegance of the table setting, the ritual of opening and tasting the wine, the unobtrusive efficiency of the waiters and their attention to detail, arranging the plates just so, whisking up bread crumbs from the tablecloth. For me, it had been a special occasion. I couldn't imagine people eating like this every day; and yet, in France, they did. It was the start of an enduring fascination with the French and their love affair with food.

# My Life in Food

## Ann Packer

THE JOY OF COOKING BEGAN, FOR ME, WITH *THE JOY OF COOKING*, its ample sections on cakes and icings. I was six or seven, and my guide was our family's housekeeper. She knew everything about baking: all the ingredients at room temperature, the difference between egg whites beaten to soft peaks and egg whites beaten to stiff peaks, what would happen when I tried to taste the delicious smell of vanilla extract. Seven-minute icing: we used a double boiler, and the sugar and egg whites transposed themselves into sweet clouds, magic on a layer cake. In second grade I loved a certain dark-haired boy, and when he consented to come home from school with me one day, we spent the warm California afternoon before his visit baking a chocolate cake and carefully carving it into the shape of a heart. The next day the boy ignored the cake and played tetherball with my brother, and I had an inkling of the fool's errands I could invent for food.

When I was fifteen a college-age friend gave me a little blue binder painted with flowers, containing lined pages for recipes. She included some of her favorites, and as this was the early 1970s these dishes bridged can cooking with Moosewood earthiness. Oatmeal Carmelitas used a jar of caramel sauce and quick-rolled oats. There was a casserole with canned corn, and there was broccoli with cheese sauce, too. I peeked outside the realm of sweets but wasn't sure I liked what I saw.

Later, a college student myself, transplanted to the East Coast, I used Christmas visits home to push my dessert making to a higher level. I advanced from a cake carved, as with the heart, into the shape of a fir tree and iced in green, to Julia Child's Bombe aux Trois Chocolats, a brownie-like cake cut to line a bowl, then filled with mousse, and, once unmolded, topped with chocolate sauce. At the approach of each holiday visit, I phoned my mother with a list of ingredients to buy before my arrival: pounds of unsalted butter, slivered almonds, apricot preserves, bittersweet Tobler or Lindt. I made Reine de Saba and Tarte aux Poires.

I moved to New York, into a studio with a tiny, separate kitchen that my uncle made usable for me by hanging a pegboard and shelves. At the publishing company where I worked, books were everywhere and free, and I carted home novels and cookbooks, Julia Child's two-volume *Mastering the Art of French Cooking*, Marcella Hazan's *Classic Italian Cookbook* and *More Classic Italian Cooking*. This was during the glossy moment of the Silver Palate, and I cooked

Chicken Monterey with orange juice and tomatoes, and wondered when I would start resembling the authors, start using their tips for entertaining and living. Would I ever have a water-side summer house to which I would welcome late-arriving guests with a Midnight at the Oasis party, complete with snifters of ouzo and dishes of dates, and Persian carpets strewn on the beach?

My rudimentary little stove alarmed me, the moment when I had to hold the lit match to the gas. It worked, though, and the blue ring cooked better than electric, sensitive to each tiny twist of the dial. I gave small dinner parties for my friends, prepared butternut squash soup and chicken with raspberries or Julia's coq au vin. I'd broken through to the meal itself, though pastry making remained my passion. Once I started work on a strawberry tart, only to be flummoxed at the custard cream by my lack of Cognac on a Sunday morning. All the liquor stores were closed, but I entered a tavern on Seventh Avenue where the bartender at first said no takeout, then sold me a snifterful that I poured into a paper cup and carried back to my fifth-floor walk-up.

It pleased me to feed people. At holiday time, I assembled small gifts of homemade mustard and cocoa-dusted truffles for my friends, the cocoa muddying my hands as I carefully rolled each ball. What was I making? A pitch for a life centered around making things? A pitch for friendship itself? I could not be forgotten while my truffles were being consumed.

Cooking bridges the gap between people, binds others to us, our food still in their stomachs as they leave us and go home to their lives. A single woman in my twenties—a single girl—I cooked a dream of adult life, of dinner parties,

which had been the center of my parents' social life: eight or
ten or sometimes sixteen men and women gathered around
a table in my childhood home, bottle after bottle of wine
going empty. On those long-ago dinner party nights, I took
an outdoor path from the kitchen to my bedroom in order to
avoid the fullness of inebriated adult life in the dining room.
Only, years later, to try it myself. Something remained elusive. One impossibly hot night my New York walk-up was
too stifling for the eight of us crowded around my table, and
we had to take my dessert to someone else's air-conditioned
apartment, where the party slipped from my grasp.

Solace came from visiting my aunt and uncle, an Amtrak
ride away. My aunt referred to herself as a burned-out cook,
but I knew better. Even breakfast had the feel of an event,
homemade or fancy bought jams set out for the English
muffins. Dinners were carefully balanced by color, texture,
and taste, usually with a special extra something that said
meals mattered: corn muffins baked in cob-shaped ironware
to go with the jambalaya, say, or beautifully puffed Yorkshire
pudding with a perfect rare roast beef. On my weekend visits
we embarked on all-day projects: Concord grape jelly made
from the purple orbs in her yard; homemade bread-and-
butter pickles, mustard seeds suspended in the vinegary liquid. I took a basket of tomatoes grown by my boss at her
house in upstate New York, and we sliced some for sandwiches on thin white bread and used the rest for a labor-
intensive sauce that tasted like liquid gold. My aunt showed
me through her cookbooks, told me about making beef
Wellington and coulibiac of salmon for special dinners, how
she'd become a cook because, in the early 1960s, she had
grown so bored with the seven-night-a-week imperative to

provide a chop, veg, and starch for her family. Watching her, I learned to cook intuitively, to add a little broth when a baking side dish began to look dry, whether the recipe suggested this or not. A gourmet is an explorer, and when she told me about a recipe for star anise beef, I cut a path to Dean & Deluca in SoHo, and on my next trip took her a brushed aluminum tin full of the woody flowers.

I got brochures for cooking schools, but when I left New York it was for the Iowa Writers' Workshop, the novels I'd hoarded taking precedence over the cookbooks. I was going to become a writer. I had an apartment in an old house on an old, cobbled street, my typewriter on a table in front of a window that looked out at a chestnut tree. I wrote and read and read and wrote, and for fun I drank gallons of beer with my fellow writers. A boyfriend and I put on a Thanksgiving dinner, using several of my aunt's Thanksgiving recipes, but there weren't enough guests and the party fell flat.

Months later, I began dating someone else. Eating, he told me with charming irony, was one of his favorite things. He bought a hibachi and I bought a blender, and we made a habit of having grilled shrimp and frozen daiquiris on the ledge outside his third-floor apartment. We invited the just-retired director of the writing program to dinner at my apartment on a humid summer night, and when I placed a half-pint of delicately washed and dried raspberries in perfect concentric circles on a cream-spread tart shell, my new boyfriend teased me about my carefulness and said his mother was interested in cooking, too. Our guests that evening had spent the day coping with the oppressive heat, our teacher's wife reporting that for relief she had lain for hours on the floor of their old house. They were moving to California, my birthplace, where the summers were dry, and I felt that moving somewhere with someone would mean the end of an uncertainty about the future by which I was so troubled that I couldn't think of it much, if at all.

A year later, this boyfriend and I moved to a new city together, and real cooking moved into the center of my life. For the two of us or for ourselves and others, I made lemon-roasted chicken and veal stew and—a recommendation from my boyfriend's mother, a wonderful cook like my aunt—slow-braised lamb shanks. We loved shrimp Diane from Paul Prudhomme, a fantasia of butter, garlic, and mushrooms. At a large brunch for friends we served homemade breakfast sausages and Grand Marnier French toast.

We married. The following summer, preparing for a year in France, we photocopied some of our favorite recipes and carefully packed measuring cups, knowing that otherwise the metric system might foil us. In the south of France we shopped daily, giving ourselves to the pleasures of tender haricots verts, fraises des bois, fresh-made pasta. At a restaurant in Normandy we sampled the great trifecta of smelly cheeses—Camembert, Livarot, and Pont-l'évêque—and we passed the self-imposed test that we like them. In the Dordogne we had our first truffles, the flavor elusive, a fleeting taste of the earth in each bite.

Back in the United States my husband entered architecture school and I gestated our first child. I was nearly finished with my first book, and I gave myself to the pregnancy, let even cooking slip away while I knit and quilted for the baby. Before she was born I cooked huge pots of some of our favorite freezable foods, Bolognese sauce, beef stew, not understanding that in cooking as in literature great themes are introduced not at once but with careful foreshadowing. Thus was born, just before our daughter, the era of batch cookery.

It lasted for years. I still cooked fresh dinners from time to time, but I had lost the ability to give myself to the preparation of a meal. Motherhood was a shocking thief of time, or I a shockingly inept multitasker. Brown chunks of lamb while the baby drummed Tupperware at my feet? It was beyond me. How much easier it was to pull a pint of Southwestern chicken casserole from the freezer and nuke it, its flavors giving way, over the course of several meals, to the taste of the freezer itself. On weekends my husband or I would make triple batches of pasta sauce or chili, but even so, as the months progressed we made do with less and less: the jambalaya without the creole sauce, the soup by itself on the table, no good bread, no salad.

Our daughter nearly rescued us. After a period of eating nothing but toaster waffles spread with cottage cheese and cut into squares, she became a culinary adventurer, and for a time I rose to the occasion. My toddler ate grilled salmon and broccoli! She ate lasagna, an affront to the first rule of toddlerdom: the foods must not touch each other! This period was not to last. And afterward, once her brother had arrived, we devolved even further, to shift eating, the kids fed at five-thirty, bathed at six-thirty, read to at seven-thirty, put to bed at eight, and the two of us looking balefully at each other across the clean kitchen counters at eight-thirty, sometimes nine, and then reluctantly opening the drawer where we kept those most important of documents, the takeout menus.

The story of how one eats is the story of how one lives: our barren, makeshift dinners signaled that something was awry. Or is it the other way around, and the cartons of chicken tikka masala would have been fine if we'd laid a tablecloth, lit candles, lingered? Chicken or egg or omelet, the takeout period marked the beginning of the end of our marriage. After much work to prevent it, and much grief in the face of it, we separated.

For the next year I served my children food I would have been appalled to own ten years earlier. I unrolled premade pizza dough and spread it with tomato sauce from a jar, then sprinkled on pregrated mozzarella. I bought Pillsbury crescent rolls and—God help me—wrapped them around hot-dog halves. We ate a lot of pancakes. We ate ramen. We ate toast. When the children were with their father I subsisted on crackers, the occasional banana. When they came back I stocked the kitchen, but somehow with food of which I disapproved, guilty-mom food: cotton candy Go-Gurts, rainbow Goldfish, Fruit Roll-Ups and s'mores Pop-Tarts. Trying to rally, I cooked tortellini, and the children pushed it away. I gruesomely under-roasted a chicken—twice in six weeks.

Meanwhile, my fantasies roved through the San Francisco restaurants I'd frequented while married. I thought of the tomato-steeped spaghetti at Delfina, the sweet and savory dragon rolls at Café Kati, the peppery shaking beef at Slanted Door. Whole meals appeared in my mind with glasses of wine beside them, mocking my recent insomnia, which had forced me to give up alcohol.

Could food ever be the thing itself, stripped of meaning and symbol and desire? One evening when the children were with their father I cooked the first real meal of my now-single life: grilled salmon, zucchini, rice. It was a turning point. I did not, of course, stop eating cereal for dinner after that, stop nuking bad enchiladas. But the future had become visible. The simple job of feeding myself could be no fool's errand: it was in fact essential. To feed myself well was to put aside regret and to say that a life changed at the halfway point could be a life saved. What had been foreshadowed with the fancy cakes thirty-five years earlier was care itself.

But to entertain is still sublime. Divorced now, I recently invited a group of friends for dinner—my first party on my own. That morning I sat at my kitchen table and shelled two pounds of English peas, my thumbnails gradually turning green as I used them to open pod after pod and then pushed the hard green globes into a bowl. Recalling the advice of an Italian friend, I bent rather than cut my asparagus stalks so that they would come apart at the natural breaking point, then discarded the woody ends and saved only the tender spears. I was making Greens' Tagliatelle with Spring Vegetables and Saffron Cream, and I measured out a quarter teaspoon of the pricey dark-orange threads and soaked them in a little boiling water to release the exotic flavor.

We were going to be seven. I added a single leaf to my table and then unfolded a cloth, spread it out, and set a bowl of flowers in the middle. The silver plate from its chest, the stemware for wine and water. In the afternoon I washed lettuce and cut segments of grapefruit and orange, having decided that citrus in the salad would be a good way to cut the richness of the main course. I left the fruit to drain and spent an hour on my bed, holding a book while in my mind I walked through the menu again, visualized the way I'd arrange the Gorgonzola and pepper crackers, reminded myself to fill a glass pitcher with ice water. Showered and

dressed, I returned to the kitchen and wiped clean my serving dishes, then put a giant pot of water on the stove and
began to heat it. When the doorbell rang, I was ready, and
we drank glasses of wine and talked while I finished my
preparations.

Is there a happier moment for a host? The work finished,
a glass of wine at hand, and all around one's table trusting
friends waiting to be fed? I don't remember now whether I
told my guests that this was a momentous dinner, but I recall
feeling both that I'd brought myself back to myself and that
I'd carried myself forward to something new.

Much later, the pasta and salad consumed, it was time for
dessert. With the table cleared, I left my friends to chat
while I returned to the kitchen. There, I set out my favorite
dessert plates, whipped cream with an electric mixer, and
gave the sugared berries one more stir. Finally, everything
else ready, I opened the cellophane bag containing the biscuits that I'd bought, not made, having learned at last that
the best solution is not always the perfect one.

# Dinner with Seamus

## Henri Cole

IN THE LATE 1990S, FOR FIVE YEARS, I TAUGHT AT HARVARD AS A lecturer in the Department of English, where Seamus Heaney was Boylston Professor of Rhetoric and Oratory. Soon after my arrival, he invited me to dinner at the Dolphin, a little seafood restaurant on Massachusetts Avenue, which he liked. He said it was to be a "social evening, not a command performance," knowing I would be nervous, and on a Tuesday after our classes, we met in the lobby of the Faculty Club to walk the few blocks to the Dolphin. The fact that he did not suggest that we eat at the Club, amid the gloomy portraits of distinguished men, indicated to me it was indeed to be a social occasion.

So, to dinner I wore blue jeans, boots, and an old fisherman's sweater that had belonged to my dead friend Bill. Seamus was wearing a plaid shirt, with an open collar, and a handsome green suit of Irish wool, which I recognized from my interview many months earlier, at which Lucie Brock-Broido, Philip Fisher, Jill McCorkle, David Perkins, and Helen Vendler, in addition to Seamus, were present. It had been a sunny January afternoon and snow was heaped on the streets. My voice cracked as I answered their questions and I had cotton mouth, but the thirty minutes went by quickly and before I knew it I was shaking everyone's hands and saying I did not wish them an easy choice, which made them all laugh, and flying home to Oregon. During the interview, Seamus asked if I preferred poets who wrote in syllabics, as I was then doing, and I replied that I liked poetry that was not like mine. His suit was exactly the color of Lucie's green eyes.

As we walked the few blocks toward the Dolphin that autumn evening, it seemed to me that everyone recognized Seamus, greeting him eagerly, and he shook their hands, listened to what they had to say, and was always polite.

When we got to the restaurant and were seated, Seamus immediately ordered a bottle of Muscadet, a dry white wine that is a fine companion to shellfish and comes from the Loire Valley, where winemakers leave grape juice after fermentation to rest during winter, before putting the wine into bottles to give it a richer flavor. Swallowing his first mouthful, Seamus said that it was his eleventh year at Harvard and he no longer felt terrified returning.

"Terrified about what?" I asked. And he replied that it was painful for him to leave his family for four months every year, and to interrupt his writing, in order to teach American students. His wife, Marie, who appears in many memorable poems, stayed on in Dublin with their young family, making it possible for Seamus to travel annually to Harvard. His friend Tomas Tranströmer, the Swedish poet, had recommended he never be apart from Marie for more than six weeks, and this was a formulation that had worked: he returned to Dublin periodically during the term.

He admitted he felt distant from American students and sometimes didn't understand where they were coming from, unlike his Irish students. But he wanted to continue teaching for six or seven more years before retiring. (In 1995 he won the Nobel Prize in Literature, which carried a purse of 7,200,000 Swedish kronor, or about 900,000 U.S. dollars today.) As he explained all this, I noticed from the corner of my eye a Cambridge poet and her husband at the next table, also listening intently. When Seamus noticed them, too, he greeted them immediately and then, without missing a beat, resumed our conversation.

To start, Seamus ordered cherrystone clams and I had a half-dozen oysters, which we ate raw, squeezing lemon juice on the creamy beige, slightly salty meat inside. A cherrystone clam is a hard-shell clam, with a thick, tough shell, and these were heart-shaped, with concentric growth lines on them, like those on a tree trunk. Cherrystones have shiny white interiors with a dark purple stain surrounding the muscle scars, and the hinges have three white teeth. They are sweeter and tenderer than larger clams; in size, they're the next step down from a quahog (pronounced CŌ-hog), a word I first learned from Walt Whitman's "Song of Myself" ("To be in any form, what is that? . . . If nothing lay more developed, the quahog and its callous shell were enough. / Mine is no callous shell . . .").

My plate of oysters made me think of Seamus's poem

called "Oysters," in which he describes them as "alive and violated," and lying on "beds of ice," and "ripped and shucked and scattered." It is the opening poem in Seamus's beautiful collection *Field Work*, which I read when I was a graduate student and was only beginning to appreciate contemporary poetry. But I was changed by it, as a growing fruit is changed by the sun.

How could I be as bold and original and astringent, I wondered?

That night at the Dolphin, when Seamus traded one of his clams for one of my oysters, it made me happy because it seemed like a gesture very much *en famille*. Later, after we had been colleagues for a couple of years, we traded fountain pens. He was autographing my copy of *Crediting Poetry*, his Nobel Lecture, with my high school Waterman pen and liked it so much I told him to keep it; in response to this, he reached in his coat pocket and gave me his nice Sheaffer, which I've never had the courage to write with, but it lies on my desk, a totem of friendship and creativity.

Seamus ordered boiled haddock for a main course, a fish I thought in keeping with his simple refinement. I, on the other hand, ordered a seafood platter, with scallops, shrimps, and a little piece of delicious cod lying together with parsley and lemon wedges on an oily white plate, an image—I laugh at myself and think—of a poet still experimenting, still becoming himself. As we ate, we talked about his new book, *The Cure at Troy*, a version of Sophocles' play *Philoctetes*, which I'd seen performed in New York City the previous spring. It had been a big success, and this brought Seamus pleasure. It was a classical play with a modern message regarding loyalty, a theme I knew to be relevant to Seamus's poetry—the loyalty to oneself versus the loyalty to one's tribe, or, to put it another way, the loyalty to personal moral beliefs versus the loyalty to political or religious callings. Of course, all poets must struggle with loyalty in order to overcome the boundaries of style, religion, race, gender and class, and national and ethnic identity, which inhibit us. Several years later, I learned that Seamus, raised a Catholic, was no longer practicing. He had, of course, long been committing himself instead to truth, or the truth of his own feelings, which is the basis of all art.

Seamus once began a lecture by thanking his colleague Helen Vendler for her introduction and adding that he always appreciated *her* truthfulness, especially when she was able to praise him. This made everyone in the audience laugh. He then went on to discuss two poems he had loved as a young man: "To a Mouse," by Robert Burns, a farmer poet, who one day turned up a mouse from its nest with his plow; the poem contemplates the destruction this wrought; and "The Yellow Bittern," by Cathal Buí Mac Giolla Ghunna, an eighteenth-century Ulster poet, who wrote in Gaelic. As on a wintry day he went walking near his home by the shores of Lough MacNean, he came upon a yellow bittern lying frozen on the ice; in his poem, Ghunna (a heavy drinker) speculates that the death was caused by the bird's not being able to drink from the iced-over water. In both poems, a man confronts a creature in nature and this confrontation yields self-awareness. Also, both poems have two powerful currents of electricity running through them, a current from the English language (caused by the friction and song of words) and another current from the human experience which language relates.

I was especially interested in Seamus's discussion because L=A=N=G=U=A=G=E poetry was very much in fashion then. It was a poetry preoccupied with fragments and unmeaning, which deranged language and eliminated connotation. Seamus seemed to be arguing that the poem of emotion *was* as important as the poem of language. This ratified me.

Recalling now the gusto with which Seamus ate his buttered haddock, I smile to myself because it is a durable fish, like him, inhabiting both the American and European coasts of the Atlantic Ocean. It feeds on most slow-moving invertebrates, including small crabs, sea worms, clams, starfish, sea cucumbers, sea urchins, and, occasionally, squid. After capture, it must be bled, gutted, and iced immediately, to retain superior flavor. The meat of the haddock is lean and white and flakes beautifully when cooked. The poetry is in the details.

When the bill for our dinner arrived, we were still eating Key lime pie. Despite protests, Seamus paid for everything, and afterward we strolled down Massachusetts Avenue to the Café Pamplona, a tiny underground coffee shop, across the street from Adams House, the college residence where Seamus lived every winter and spring. It was smoky and claustrophobic but rather appealing, too, and later, I occasionally met honors students there for conferences. Seamus was flying to Kentucky the next morning but didn't seem to want our evening to end, suggesting we even go for a Jack Daniel's after an espresso. Heading for the bar, we passed still another local poetry figure, walking his dog, and Seamus informed me he was one of the strings that, once plucked, made the whole harp of literary Cambridge tremble. He wanted me to take this under advisement, and I did.

Over the years, I took many things he said under advisement. When I published my fourth collection of poetry, *The Visible Man*, I was worried it would be narrowly defined by its gay content, but Seamus objected, using the word *arena*— the arena of human emotion, he called it—which is where all good poems must operate, rather than catering to special interests. The arena of human emotion was where my poems would find a place, he insisted, because the feelings in them were familiar to us all and because the language had a complex geology. I didn't expect this from the son of an Irish cattle dealer.

On another occasion, seeking advice about teaching, I told Seamus I didn't want to compete against the poets of my generation for the few desirable positions at American universities.

"It would take an almost unnatural purity to succeed without teaching," he replied, emphasizing that he'd been lucky to find a half-year arrangement, giving him eight months of writing time each year.

And when he visited my undergraduate poetry writing class, he told a student who complained about being from Salem, Oregon, where'd she'd grown up in a bookless, media-dominated environment, that most fine writers were from disadvantaged backgrounds and this, in and of itself, wasn't an excuse for not succeeding. This of course did *not* surprise me, coming as it did from a scholarship boy, the eldest of nine children, who'd grown up on a small farm in a country of posted soldiers.

That night at the Pamplona, we ordered espressos, and the shiny stainless-steel espresso machine whistled in the background. Steam forced through roasted and powdered coffee beans makes a shrieking sound, like truth. Our coffee was served with little glasses of water on the side and a small pyramid of sugar packets. In one of my earliest childhood memories, I am three and sitting at a table in Marseille, France, with my grandmother, eating a warm croissant and dunking it in her bowl of café au lait. It is adulthood I taste then, and that I still taste now whenever I drink an espresso. In fact, I'm writing this on a damp gray morning in Paris and drinking an espresso, while feeling a river of other things Seamus said flood through me.

# The Longest Hour

## Margot Livesey

### I. HATEFUL MEALS

OF ALL THE ELABORATE FANTASIES I HAD AS A CHILD ABOUT LIFE as a grown-up, the only one that has come true, so far, is that I get to eat what I want. Or more precisely, when I am faced with dismal choices in airports, for instance, or hotels, I get to not eat what I don't want. Throughout my childhood, meals were not battlegrounds—which might as least have offered the thrill of skirmishes and retreats, feints and maneuvers, wounds freshly given or received—but sieges; and I was always the beleaguered. Ironically, it was the presence of food, rather than its absence, that created this painful condition. Years later, reading Alistair Horne's *The Fall of Paris: The Siege and the Commune 1870–71*, I was struck less by the eloquent descriptions of starvation, than by Horne's account of how the desperate Parisians dispatched first carrier pigeons, then snails, to carry messages out of the city and across enemy lines. But I had no way I could send a message; no one to send it to.

My principal, although not my sole, adversary in this struggle was my stepmother. Janey had grown up with three siblings and a widowed father in a croft in the northeast of Scotland. I have a tiny photograph of the four children standing beside a horse and cart on an overcast, windy day. All four are scowling, and the dresses and long hair of the girls are blowing in the wind; my stepmother is barefoot. The children walked several miles to school daily, in all weathers. They came home to stack the peat, feed the hens, weed the garden, help in the fields, mind the sheep, and milk the cows. When they sat down to meals they said grace and ate what they were given. The older daughter stayed home to care for her widowed father. Janey chose one of the few professions open to women of her class: nursing. She spent most of her adult life, until she married my father, living in hostels and eating whatever the dining room served. Suddenly, in her early fifties for the first time she had a home and a kitchen of her own, a husband and a stepdaughter to feed.

This feeding had to be accomplished within the constraints of our lives at the boys' school where my father taught. The school was in a valley about fifty miles north of Edinburgh and was surrounded by farms, bare hills, and moors. The nearest shops were in the village four miles away—a journey that no one, after a decade of petrol rationing, made casually. Most of our food was purchased from the vans that circled the valley, visiting outlying houses: the butcher and the greengrocer came twice a week, the fishmonger only on Friday. Milk was delivered and bread was brought up from the village.

Once the food entered our house it had to be stored and then cooked. Bell's Cottage had a larder with a gray marble slab but no refrigerator. Both custom and climate made this less problematic than it would be nowadays. The school had fridges but no one we knew had one at home, and heat waves were rare; it's boiling, we complained, when the temperature reached seventy. Just as well, given that all cooking was done on the Esse, a solid black stove, fed with coke twice a day. Esse was a creature of moods, faltering and flaring with the winds; dishes emerged barely cooked, or done to a crisp. If she went out she took a long while to recover. On winter mornings, when ice glazed our windows, inside and out, Janey and I would dress in the small circle of her warmth; I would marvel at Janey's corset, like a suit of armor, only worn beneath the clothes.

My father, who had spent his entire adult life in schools, was of that generation of men who could barely make a cup of tea and were proud of the fact. A slice of toast was the far frontier of gourmet cooking. He was, of course, in charge of alcoholic beverages. So it was just as well that Janey, in spite of her institutional life, was a competent cook. Only now, as I write this, do I realize that I have no sense of whether she enjoyed cooking. Probably that was not a question that women of her generation asked as three times a day, seven days a week, they set the table; restaurants were a rare treat, takeaway and prepared meals unknown. Janey had learned to cook from her older sister in the Scottish tradition. She baked scones, she made pancakes—not for breakfast but for afternoon tea—about two inches in diameter and eaten cold with butter and raspberry jam. She made meringues (particularly vulnerable to Esse's whims) and a lovely, light Victoria sponge. Very occasionally she made gingerbread. Afternoon tea was my favorite meal. I could eat as little, but not as much, as I wanted. And the grown-ups tolerated my presence as they sat around the fireplace in the sitting room.

So was the siege one of pleasure? Alas, no. To reach tea, I had to survive the main meal of the day, which at that time was lunch. For lunch, six days a week, Janey cooked and served meat. The concept of vegetarianism was unknown in our world, although, among my father's books, I did discover a novel by Aldous Huxley that included a vegetarian couple, pitable, pale, sandal-wearing people who tried to feed their dog on oatmeal. For Janey, people who didn't eat meat were poor. We were not poor. Quod erat demonstrandum. She remarked often, and joyfully, that she had married a gentleman.

My dislike of meat, I should explain, was based on taste rather than principle. I loved animals but accepted unthinkingly the ruthless economy of the farm. As an adult, I was pleased to discover other vegetarians, but I have often felt embarrassed by my own less robust principles. There was no element of sacrifice in my not eating meat, and my aversion was, at least partly, the result of geography. The summer I was eighteen, I went to Paris as an au pair. The city had long emerged from its various sieges and the family I worked for was intrigued by my not eating meat. One evening, Monsieur, a doctor, put on his apron and cooked a piece of veal with butter and mushrooms. The whole family gathered to watch me eat. The meat was delicious, tender, succulent. I could tell from the first mouthful that if I had grown up in

France I would have been a carnivore, but somehow it was too late. Years of forcing down lukewarm mutton and stringy beef had made it impossible to reverse my tastes. I tried to explain this in my pedestrian French. The family nodded, not reproachfully but sadly; I was missing out on one of life's exquisite pleasures.

Of all the rooms at Bell's Cottage I have the least vivid memories of the kitchen—perhaps because I spent so many unhappy hours there. Like other children I knew, I didn't eat with my parents. So I sat alone at the table. Only on very special occasions was I allowed to read. With no one to talk to, nothing else to do, I had just one task: to clean my plate. But this often involved hard choices. Should I eat the things I liked—assuming there were any—alone, or was it better to use them as a kind of camouflage for the meat, thereby rendering the former less likeable and the latter only faintly more so? Was it better to struggle through the meat while the nice food cooled, or to eat the nice things first and then approach the dingy slices? While I wrestled with these dilemmas, Janey came and went, correcting my manners and urging me to eat up. I could not leave the table until my plate was empty (India, starving children, the trouble she had gone to on my ungrateful behalf). I remember sitting there for hours, staring at the increasingly cold, increasingly unappetizing food. Probably it was more like half an hour, three-quarters at most.

My only, unreliable, ally in these struggles was the family dog, a sweet-natured border terrier named Speckie. Sometimes she loitered, obligingly, under the table and I could slip her a piece of meat. Too often, alas, she was out in the garden chasing the rabbits that plagued my father's vegetables. So I sat there, cutting the meat into smaller and smaller pieces, washing down each piece, unchewed, with water. From this point of view mince was obviously the best, mutton and beef the worst—no, liver was the worst. Leopold Bloom's appreciation of offal is the one part of *Ulysses* I have never been able to appreciate. On the grimmest days the main course would be preceded by oxtail soup, which I detested, and followed by one of the few desserts I loathed: tapioca.

Matters improved, in some sense, when I started school. I had my main meal there and when I got home had only a sandwich before homework and bed. No one asked about, and I didn't mention, the school's inflexible version of Janey's principles. We had to finish everything on our plates and there was no choice about what that was, so if the main course was, say, potatoes, carrots, and mutton, I ate nothing. Led by our headmistress, we raced through grace: "For what we are about to receive may the Lord make us truly thankful. Amen." Then I sat down to play with my cutlery. Was I too young, I wonder, to appreciate the irony? Although the pupils were weighed at the beginning and end of each term, no one noticed that I regularly lost fifteen pounds. I regained the weight during the holidays when, once again, Janey was watching over me.

There are a remarkable number of meals in a week, a month, a year, but eventually I became a teenager and attended a different school, where I could take a packed lunch. I made it myself every evening, exactly the same for five years: a sandwich of pasteurized cheese with Janey's rhubarb chutney, a cox's apple, two biscuits, and a small thermos of instant coffee. But every silver cloud has a dark lining. I was now deemed sufficiently mature to eat with my parents in the evening. Or perhaps it was just too much trouble to have me eat separately.

By this time we were living in a farmhouse that we rented for a very modest sum. From the outside the house was attractive, the gray stone covered with Virginia creeper, a sloping garden with a copper beech and mature rhododendrons. Inside I remember one ugly room after another, and the ugliest room was the one where we spent the most time: the living room, which contained the television—a fairly recent acquisition—and the dreaded dining room table. We no longer had an Esse, and Janey produced our meals in the scullery using a little electric stove called a Baby Belling, of which she was very proud: it was reliable, modern, clean. The Baby sat on top of another modern acquisition, a formica-topped table. For power cuts and larger meals there was also a gas ring, fueled by a cylinder. Still, no fridge.

The French writer André Gide claimed that the happiest and the saddest hours of our lives pass at exactly the same rate. I beg to differ. These interminable suppers lasted from seven p.m. to, say, 7:25, and no hours in my life, however anxious, however difficult, however joyful, however sad, have passed more slowly. I was responsible for laying the table; my father sat at the head, Janey and I on either side. She served the food in the kitchen and I carried in the plates. No one said grace. My father's inevitable compliment—I wish I could remember his exact phrase—took the place of that.

Nor do I remember much of our conversations. Topics that occurred almost nightly would include the weather (Scottish and changeable), the birds that visited the bird feeder, any other flora and fauna, and one or two items from the six o'clock news. Although my father and stepmother were a devoted couple, conversation often faltered. I don't know why. Perhaps it was my fault, although I do remember doing my best: in Latin we had read about beekeeping, in history the Corn Laws were just about to be repealed. I still cut the meat into tiny pieces and had become expert at making my water last until the final piece was gone. Periodically Janey broached the alarming theory that drinking with meals was bad for the digestion but I always filled the glasses to the brim. They came from my grandfather's vicarage and I have them still, my twelve, staunch allies. The new family dog was irascible and no help whatsoever.

I ate dinner with my parents most nights for the next four years, and during that time, for reasons that had little to do with food, meals grew steadily harder; a graph plotting conviviality and pleasure would have sloped gently but inexorably from low to lower. My father had retired from teaching and both his appetite and his stock of conversation dwindled. "Oh, Toby," Janey would say as he set aside his plate unfinished, "I don't know why I bother." As for me, I fled the table as soon as I could to do the washing up and return to my homework. I worked on the card table in the parlor, where the wallpaper depicted, over and over, galleons in full sail at sunset. I remember now with some surprise that the phone sat in one corner; it was used so seldom it had to be dusted. Only when my parents were safely in bed did I venture upstairs to my L-shaped room. In the morning I left for school without seeing them. It was no surprise when I won the school medal, beating several girls with happier home lives.

*Menu for a Miserable Meal, recipes not provided*

Oxtail soup

Boiled potatoes, not new, no butter allowed

Boiled cabbage or mashed turnip—ditto

Slice of mutton with gravy, or lamb perhaps with homemade mint sauce

Tapioca

One glass of water

## II. HAPPY MEALS

But I was not always asking for less; sometimes, and not only at tea, I wanted more. Sometimes Janey would buy a little tin of macaroni and cheese from the butcher and that would be my main course. Sometimes she made fish cakes, which I loved and was allowed to eat with ketchup. Sometimes my father's bachelor friends came to supper and I, still not worthy to eat with the grown-ups when there was company, was allowed to have a cheese sandwich, my second of the day, and later eat the leftover sherry trifle. I used to make it for my North American friends until they discovered cholesterol. On Shrove Tuesdays Janey made crepes, beautifully thin, which we ate with lemon juice and sugar. She was adept at tossing them and I pictured her effortlessly winning one of the pancake races that were mentioned in the newspaper on Ash Wednesday.

That summer in Paris when I was eighteen, one of my duties was to go to the local market armed with a list that Annie, the maid, had written. I still remember the shock of those stalls: the tomatoes were so red and fragrant, the peaches so golden, the mushrooms so smooth and white, the asparagus so elegant. I stared in admiration at the gleaming mounds of butter, the pyramids of eggs, glowing as if lit from within, the rounds of cheese, firm or dimpled. Almost always I bought too much. Annie would tut-tut when she saw how little money and how much produce I brought home. I couldn't explain that I wanted more, more. Food, I was discovering, could be about pleasure, about affection.

Janey cooked meat and forced me to eat it because she had grown up that way; because she knew of no alternative; because she believed that it was good for me; because it was too much trouble to do anything else. Did she enjoy watching me, day after day, shrink from my plate? I don't know. But I do know that sometimes, not often, she cooked to please me and that I always thanked her ardently.

I am living in Iowa City this autumn and, for some reason, as I write this essay, I have been dreaming about my father and my stepmother night after night. I never meet them in these dreams; I am always looking. Perhaps these nightly visitations will stop now that I've finished this essay; perhaps they won't. But somehow these dreams have made it clear to me what may not be clear in these pages. If I could have found a snail to carry a message from me to Janey it would have been a very short one: love me.

### Menu for a Happy Meal

Tomato soup, tinned—see Andy Warhol

Fish cakes—see recipe below

Peas—freshly picked or tinned, no matter

New potatoes, straight from my father's garden, with butter and mint

Rhubarb crumble with custard—substitute gooseberries in season

# My Stepmother's Fish Cakes, with Some Variations

I serve these with mayonnaise to which I've added the zest and juice of 2 limes.

    1 pound potatoes
    1 pound salmon (Janey always used tinned salmon)
    fish stock, wine, or milk, for poaching the salmon
    Salt and pepper
    4 spring onions
    ½ red bell pepper
    1 teaspoon dill
    2 teaspoons capers
    2 eggs
    seasoned flour (seasoned with salt and pepper)
    bread crumbs
    vegetable or canola oil, for frying

**SERVES 4:** Boil the potatoes. While the potatoes are cooking, poach the salmon in fish stock, wine, or milk. Finely chop the spring onions, bell pepper, and dill. Mash the potatoes and season with salt and pepper. Add the spring onions, bell pepper, dill, and capers. Then add the salmon, taking care to keep the fish in flakes. Shape this mixture into cakes. Dip each cake in beaten egg, then in the seasoned flour, in the beaten egg again, and in the bread crumbs. Fry or grill on each side until browned.

# A Feast of Preparations

## David Lehman

IT MAY BE HERESY IN THIS CONTEXT TO CONFESS, BUT I DON'T much like giving or even attending dinner parties. Too many things can go wrong, even beyond the possibility of a disaster in the kitchen sabotaging the meal. A couple whose marriage is on the rocks will choose this occasion to rehearse their resentments. A neglected spouse will get soused and say nasty things about broadcast journalism despite knowing that the hostess holds an executive position with one of the networks. A bore will launch an interminable rant, the burden of which is that free agency has killed baseball the way rock 'n' roll killed jazz and therefore American culture sucks and it's *your* fault. A provocateur of either sex will try to get a rise out of the group by declaring, with regard to the attacks of September 11, that we had it coming. Or someone will call someone else a racist, a fascist, or a

Republican, take your pick. Or perhaps a perfectly nice stranger will have brought a manuscript of poems hoping that I will recommend it for publication, blurb it, and write a letter of recommendation to the Guggenheim Foundation. I speak from experience. These things happen.

Yet I know that the truth is more complicated and that I could only have written the paragraph above in the cranky mood I'm currently in because my old trusty Toyota died on a country road this morning and I waited two hours for AAA to arrive and it's eleven degrees today with snow flurries and brisk winds and I have two deadlines to meet and there's no food in the house. That's where I'm coming from, and it isn't a pretty place. On the other hand I find that two jiggers of Knob Creek bourbon, half a jigger of Chambord liqueur, and a lot of ice will make the deadlines seem much more manageable, so in approved post-modernist fashion let me avail myself of such remedy—an improvement on the standard Manhattan (whiskey and sweet vermouth)—and start this piece all over, beginning with the beginning. Ah yes, that's better.

It was a lovely September evening a month after Stacey and I were married by a judge before two witnesses in upstate New York, Stacey quoting Sammy Cahn ("Time after time / I tell myself that I'm / So lucky to be loving you") and I opting for Johnny Mercer ("For you are the lover I have waited for, / the mate that fate had me created for"). It was a half hour after a reading at the New School in New York City featuring no fewer than twenty contributors to *The Best American Poetry 2005* as well as that book's guest editor (Paul Muldoon) and series editor (yours truly). The event attracted a big crowd and went well. We even had a surprise for the audience, a last-minute addition to the program: John Ashbery, my favorite poet and many people's candidate for the foremost poet in the land. The poets read their work with charm and conviction and amazingly no one exceeded his or her allotted time at the lectern.

To celebrate we went to the Café Loup, where Robert Polito, who heads the New School's writing program, generously decided to underwrite an impromptu dinner party for all the evening's participants. Stacey was there; John Ashbery was there with his companion, David Kermani; lots of other poets were there including my friend Mark Bibbins, and we were sipping Tanqueray martinis (straight up, with olives) and feeling fine. I was seated next to John Ashbery, so I was even happier with my lot in life, and I must have been bragging about Stacey's culinary prowess, because John—a gastronome of the highest order, who, when he lived in Paris as a young man, thought nothing of crossing the city to sample some obscure restaurant's house specialty—grew animated. I had a sudden inspiration. Would John and David come to dinner? Done!

In the time-honored male manner I elected to leave the planning entirely to my wife. Stacey loves spending time with John and David, and the prospect of planning a princely menu excited her. Still, it didn't take long for an element of dread to surface. Although she loves to cook, and I think she's exceptional, Stacey would describe herself as merely a "decent home cook," meaning she can get a healthy simple dinner on the table mid-week in under an hour. But when it comes to entertaining, she is seriously out of practice. Ever since moving to New York City in 1998 she has curtailed her entertaining because of the limits imposed by a small apartment with a tiny kitchen and no dishwasher.

We live on the top floor of a six-floor walk-up, eighty steps from ground level, far too many for John, now seventy-eight, to climb. So where could we hold the dinner? I thought of Mark Bibbins, who lives with his tech-whiz companion Brian in a spacious Chelsea apartment with a wraparound porch. Like Stacey, Mark loves to cook and is very good at it, and he, too, is very fond of John and David. Mark and Brian agreed to collaborate with us, and after a flurry of e-mails with all parties, we settled on a Sunday night in November, the thirteenth to be exact, and we were in business. That was two months in the future. I entered the information in my calendar and did my best to forget about it, which was just as well: Stacey proved herself capable of obsessing enough for two.

About a week later, Stacey proposed the broad outlines of a menu to Mark. The centerpiece would be her specialty, a dish she has prepared often enough that it's practically a guaranteed success: braised lamb shanks. Unfortunately, Mark replied with the news that he does not eat red meat. As far as he could tell, Stacey took this news in stride, assuring him that an alternative would be easy to figure out. In reality, however, panic set in, but panic of the productive kind, fueled by adrenaline, or so it seemed to this observer.

A frenzy of menu planning and recipe testing ensued. It was as if Stacey were Carême cooking for the Romanovs in Saint Petersburg. She consulted the many cookbooks and cooking magazines she owns. She visited online recipe sources. She phoned friends. Just as at any given moment during a movie, or while attending a reading, I might be spied counting iambs on my fingers, or scribbling furiously in my notebook, Stacey would jot down menu options at odd moments. I found scraps of paper with cooking notes and shopping lists throughout our tiny apartment; on the desk, the kitchen cabinet, the coffee table. When she confessed her anxieties, I spoke my own lines as if veteran sitcom writers had scripted them for me: "Relax, sweetie. Anything you make will be wonderful."

Stacey's requirements were few but non-negotiable. First, she wanted the meal to have a decidedly French accent. She had told John about mastering several recipes from Patricia Wells's first edition of her *Food Lover's Guide to Paris*; he was especially attentive to Stacey's description of a hazelnut praline soufflé she recalled eating in 1983 at a restaurant in the eighteenth *arrondissement*. She imagined her cooking inducing a nostalgic swoon: "This reminds me of the *daube* Frank O'Hara and I had at a cute bistro on the Rue du Bac in 1960."

Second, she wanted to be able to prepare the main dish in advance so that once the guests arrived, she wouldn't be distracted by the goings on in Mark's open kitchen. Cooking while others watch makes her nervous. She didn't want anyone peering over her shoulder while she tried to rescue a separating hollandaise or repair—gasp!—overcooked vegetables.

Finally, she wanted the meal to be elegant but casual, and seemingly effortless, as if she regularly whipped up such meals at a moment's notice. Ideally, the entire evening would unfold as a marvel of spontaneity, with one glorious dish after another marching from kitchen to table. "Dinner for six, dear? No sweat. I'll pull something together."

My theory of a good dinner party is that much depends on the quality of the opening cocktails, and so I volunteered to take responsibility for this part of the meal. What to serve? Martinis were reliable but unimaginative; daiquiris were delicious, but I associate them with summer. My solution was to serve Bellinis. It's not a difficult drink to make. You simply add peach brandy to good but inexpensive nonvintage Champagne. It's even better if you use white peach purée in addition to the brandy, and I knew that Stacey had frozen some that she had made in August using peaches from the farmers' market in Ithaca, where we spend much of the summer. What's more, I had recently discovered Mathilde Liqueur Pêches, a superb peach liqueur imported from France. The combination of these ingredients was sure to put everyone in a mood the opposite of which was mine when I sat down to write this piece a few hours ago.

Stacey's theory of successful entertaining, much less liquid, is that it takes only one spectacular dish to impress the guests and leave the impression of complete kitchen mastery. If the dish is served at the beginning of the meal, it will prejudice the guests in favor of everything that follows. If it comes at the end, the diners will forget any preceding mediocrity. Everything else can be plain, as long as it tastes okay. One *horrid* dish will spoil everything.

Stacey's consultations with Mark continued. They agreed that duck in some fashion might make a good entrée. The only problem was that Stacey had never cooked duck. It wasn't part of her cooking lexicon. Nevertheless, she gave it a shot. A vendor at the Wednesday farmers' market on Chambers Street, near her office in Lower Manhattan, sells free-range fowl of all kinds. One day, as I mounted the stairs to our apartment, I heard a shrill alarm that grew louder with each flight until I realized it was coming from our home. Wisps of smoke curled out from under the front door. And there on a stepladder stood Stacey, screwdriver in hand, trying to disable the alarm. The shriveled carcass of the duck sat on the counter.

The duck breasts were a different story. They were delicious and they accommodated a variety of sauces. But they failed in both the prepare-in-advance and elegant-but-casual categories. Stacey does great things with chicken or seafood and rice dishes—paella, jambalaya—but these lacked the specifically French character she wanted the meal to have. Bouillabaisse? More suited to summer, she felt. Simple roast chicken? "Hasn't that become a cliché?" Game hens with soy-citrus glaze, chicken breasts over wild mushrooms, whole fish baked in a salt crust: for one reason or another, Stacey rejected all these and others.

I noticed that Stacey, when cooking, had taken to wearing a smock-like garment with ruffles and heart-shaped pockets, the kind you would see plump women wearing in old *Life* magazine advertisements for Campbell's soup. When I asked her about it she explained that its provenance was the Sixth Avenue flea market and that it gave her confidence. "I feel like Mary Tyler Moore's Laura Petrie to Dick Van Dyke's Rob. The wife cooking to impress her husband's boss."

A different analogy occurred to me. Immersed as I was in writing an essay on Hitchcock for *American Heritage* magazine, I must ungallantly admit that I thought of Mrs. Oxford in *Frenzy*, who creates exotic but scary French dishes often involving an animal's innards, which her long-suffering

husband, the Chief Inspector, pretends to enjoy while longing for roast beef and Yorkshire pudding.

In truth Stacey's nervousness was understandable. You
see, Ashbery is the one person I know well whom I consider
a genius. As a poet I owe much to his example, and as a jour-
nalist too: I reviewed books for *Newsweek* while John was
the art critic there. When I launched *The Best American
Poetry* in 1988 with the idea that a different guest editor,
himself or herself a distinguished poet, would choose the
contents each year, I asked John to serve as the guest editor
of the inaugural volume. Not only did he select the poems
and contribute a terrific introduction, but he also helped me
create the template for the structure of subsequent volumes
in the series.

Knowing the depth of my dedication to John, Stacey—
herself a long-time admirer of John's work—has come up
with imaginative ways for us to celebrate our friendship with
him. When Stacey and I went to Paris in 1998, we photographed the various apartment houses where John had lived
during his ten-year Paris sojourn, and on our return we made
an album and gave it to him. This was Stacey's idea. And
on her birthday in 2003 we drove from Ithaca to Sodus,
the rural village near Rochester where John grew up, and
photographed the still-remaining "Ashbery Farms" sign near
the corner of Maple Avenue and Lake Road. Later, John and
David told us that they themselves made a pilgrimage to
Sodus as a result of the photos we sent to them.

There is something about John that inspires people to
want to do things for him. Perhaps it is just our gratitude for
his presence—our love of his poems—or perhaps this is part

of his personal charm, along with his reticence and his sometimes enigmatic and frequently brilliant off-the-cuff aphorisms. He has said that he feels poems are "going on all the time in my head and I occasionally snip off a length." On spotting a difficult friend: "There goes B., wearing her resentments like an egret." On going his own way: "Very often people don't listen to you when you talk to them. It's only when you talk to yourself that they prick up their ears."

And both Stacey and I are tremendously fond of David, John's companion for more than three decades. David is devoted to John in the customary sense of that phrase but with a scholar's thoroughness and integrity. As a young librarian at Columbia, David prepared a comprehensive bibliography of John's works, which was published in 1976. It's an exemplary volume, and I have no doubt that the Ashbery Resource Center, which David has established, will prove a treasure trove for future scholars. Stacey thinks of David as a role model of sorts and has learned much from him about being the partner of a public figure. He is also the kind of person one would want to be seated beside at a formal dinner, an excellent conversationalist with an insatiable curiosity and an offbeat sense of humor. His opinion mattered to both of us.

At dinner one evening (seared tuna steaks with wasabi sauce, confit of sweet red and green pepper, and wild rice), Stacey announced that she had made a decision. With the aplomb of William Powell fingering the culprit in the climactic dinner scene in *The Thin Man*, she declared that she had figured out what to serve: coq au vin. She ticked off the reasons. She had made it before, and while it's not her fa-vorite dish, she knew she could pull it off with a really good wine and "cipolline onions instead of those tiny boiling onions that take forever to peel." If Mark would agree to allow a tiny bit of bacon for flavoring, there you had it. Coq au vin! It may seem anticlimactic to you, dear reader, but it made us happy.

This, then, was the menu:

Bellinis

Cheese Gougères

Endive Spears with Marjoram Pesto

Mark's Crab Cakes with Corn Salsa

Coq au Vin

Roasted New Potatoes

Homemade Crusty Rolls

Mark's Green Salad with Sherry Vinaigrette

Nougat Glacé with Raspberry Sauce

With entrée settled, Stacey proceeded to perfect the three dishes she was counting on to establish her reputa-tion: the *gougères,* the homemade rolls, and the nougat glacé. She had made these dishes many times in her pre–New York City days, but, like any smart cook, wanted to refresh her skills. She liked the *gougères*—simple, bite-size savory puff pastries, served warm—because they're de-licious and pretty and seem to require an element of magic. The homemade rolls were an obvious choice. Stacey is an experienced baker who used to work on a cooperative farm in Williamstown, Massachusetts; while we were courting, she baked a braided challah, froze it, and shipped it to me so that it would arrive ready to eat. As for the nougat glacé, it's rarely seen on restaurant menus in the U.S. though it's fairly common in France. It's a sensual delight, a soft frozen confection studded with slivered almonds and pistachios that sits in a pool of raspberry purée. Whoever invented it—and there are several apocryphal tales—was inspired by the nougat candy comprising egg whites, almonds, pistachios, and lavender honey that has its origins in the Provençal town of Montelimar. It's Stacey's favorite dessert. Years earlier she had gone to great lengths to master it. In her kitchen she tried to duplicate the epiphany of the nougat glacé she had tasted at La Chancelière during a long-ago bicycle trip through the Loire Valley. After many mishaps, she achieved success when *Gourmet* magazine published a recipe from the very restaurant where the dessert had been served to her.

While Stacey went in pursuit of menu perfection, I thought little of the event until it was almost upon us. But I had an ace up my sleeve. Ever since last summer I have been making mixed-media collages and watercolor drawings, many of them in standard postcard size. There are high-quality art supply stores where I live, and the practice of making these art works—while perhaps a crime drama airs on TV or Sinatra sings on FM radio—relaxes me. I have never done anything of the sort before, and I am sure I would have dropped the habit if the first or second or even the fifth person to whom I showed the collages had made a belittling remark or laughed derisively. To my amazement and pleasure everyone seems to like the works, including John, who had earned his living as an art critic from his Paris days when he reviewed museum and gallery exhibitions for the *International Herald Tribune*.

A day before the blessed event I made something for everyone. For Brian, I juxtaposed a newspaper photo of Marilyn Monroe with crossed-out lines of handwritten poetry and stripes of white and yellow on a crossword-puzzle background. For David, I painted a luminous red moon and other things on a photograph of the New York City skyline on the night of the blackout of 1965, a November night like this one. (It was in fact the night before John Ashbery landed in New York after living in France for the better part of the previous ten years.) For John, who gave the title *Your Name Here* to a recent collection of his poems, I glued a photo of the Italian mannerist painter Francesco Parmigianino— whose *Self-Portrait in a Convex Mirror* inspired Ashbery's most famous single poem—to a fake American Express card made out to "your name here." For Mark, who had distributed handsome silver matchbooks with *Sky Lounge* in black lettering on them when his book of that title was published, I made the matchbook the centerpiece of a collage. And for Stacey, I made an homage to Greta Garbo and bought a CD consisting of dance music by Harold Arlen, Richard Rodgers, and Cole Porter, which we would play that evening during the dinner. When the meal began, the collages in envelopes with the diners' names on them would be on each person's plate like an eccentric form of place cards.

At four-thirty in the afternoon it occurred to me that I had not planned a toast. I like a challenge, and instead of a conventional toast, I decided to write one in the form of a sestina.* I allocated one hour to the task, and this is what I came up with:

### Dinner Party Sestina

The caller demanded to speak to John.
"He isn't here." "Who's this?" "This is David."
"David?" "Yes, but not that David."
"Oh." "I can see you're an easy mark."
"Forgive me." "OK, but don't tell Brian."
"Brian left to buy Champagne," said Stacey.

The gang gathered around Stacey
the way poets at a reading gather around John.
"He isn't here." "Who's this?" "This is O'Brien
and you're Winston Smith." "Quit it, David,"
whose penchant for one-liners and unremark-
able puns was noted by all. And in walked David

himself, looking less like Michelangelo's David
each year, but happy now that he married Stacey.
"It seems that Cupid's arrow hit the mark," Mark
said, not unself-referentially. Moments passed. "Hi, John,"
said a lovesick sheriff searching for a walnut, but Brian
set him straight. "If he's John, I'm David."

---

*As may or may not be self-evident from this example, the sestina form consists of thirty-nine lines distributed across seven stanzas, six of six lines each and a closing triplet. The same six words end all the lines, recurring in a predetermined order.

"And if I'm John, he's David," said David,
looking up from reading Elizabeth David's
Provençal cookbook on loan from Brian,
who had previously borrowed it from Stacey.
"Has anyone brought a poem—I mean besides John?"
"And the twayne shall not converge," said Mark,

a mystifying but nonetheless satisfying remark.
Everyone wondered how David
would respond. But David said nothing. John
took out an old Firesign Theater record to show David
who said, "not now," and raised a toast to Stacey,
author of the meal chez Mark and Brian.

As brain is an anagram of Brian,
(I told Mark)
"yes cat" is an anagram of Stacey,
and there is a diva in every David,
though not every David
can be as avid as the day he first met John

on the page, in a sestina in which Popeye
cavorting with his crew stood for John
and David, Mark, Brian, Stacey, and the other David.

It was thrilling to write it, and to write it so swiftly, but
when the moment came I uncharacteristically lost the nerve
to read it. Instead I gave or e-mailed a copy to each person
present on the following day.

The evening was beautiful, unseasonably warm, and
when I arrived, sestina folded in jacket pocket, Stacey and

Mark were in the kitchen, and the most wonderful aroma of wine and caramelized onion wafted in the air. Stacey was piping *pâte à choux* onto a baking sheet for the *gougères*, Mark was misting the tablecloth with water to smooth the wrinkles, and Brian was checking the sound system and loading his play list. Once Mark finished setting the table, I placed an envelope with collage inside on each plate. And then we waited nervously for John and David to show up. We started on the Bellinis. I sampled the endive spears with marjoram pesto. Magnificent. Then the doorbell rang and there were David and John with two bottles of Champagne (Piper-Heidsieck, brut). We ate the *gougères* on the terrace. Rather than sauté the crab cakes as he usually does, Mark tossed them into a deep fryer, and rued the decision when muffled popping sounds issued from the kitchen. But the diners were oblivious to the noise and the crab cakes made a marvelous appetizer. Stacey worried that her coq au vin was too dry, especially the breasts, but it was popular with our guests. I had a leg and a thigh, which are the parts of the chicken that benefit most from being cooked slowly with an ample quantity of wine, mushrooms, onions, black pepper, and garlic. I loved it—I love bistro cooking in general—and happily had seconds.

I remember little else of the occasion except that Mark took photographs with the tiniest digital camera I have ever seen and Stacey's dessert was a heavenly highlight and John and Mark watch the Food Network as does Stacey, and all have opinions about the relative talents of Rachael Ray, Giada De Laurentiis, and Emeril. Stacey talked about our recent trip to Poland, and David talked about trips he and John have made to far-flung places, and Brian turned out to be a music aficionado, and we talked about the dance music on the CD we had brought and played, and John said that he had met Balanchine and he also commented admiringly on Emma McCagg's portrait of Mark hanging on his foyer wall. Mark reminds me that while sipping cocktails and eating hors d'oeuvres on the terrace, John spotted "two of my neighbors in the act of sharing some horizontal affection. We've lived in the building for three years and never witnessed such a show. Maybe they knew he was coming." A profile on John had appeared a few weeks earlier in *The New Yorker*, and when we talked about that, John said there was only one thing that concerned him and that was that his landlord would read the article and try to evict him for maintaining a residence in Hudson, New York. Everyone liked his or her present, and when the time came to clink glasses, John toasted Stacey and me "for getting married so we could have this celebration." We couldn't have asked for anything more.

## STACEY'S NOUGAT GLACÉ

The poet Jim Cummins is joining us for dinner tonight and I've decided to make this dessert again because it is always a success, can be made a day or two in advance if necessary, and lends itself to many variations. It's basically a soft ice cream; the Italian version is called a semifreddo and there are many different recipes for it, some with whole eggs, others with just yolks, as well as this version, which uses only the whites. I like it because the end result is closer in color to the nougat candy that inspired its creation (the crème de cassis gives it a faint pink blush). And I also like beating the egg whites in the beautiful copper mixing bowl I recently found at the local thrift shop for ten dollars.

The tricky part of the glacé is the Italian meringue, which is more complicated to pull off than other kinds of meringue, such as the kind used to top a lemon meringue pie. It requires using a candy thermometer and boiling sugar and water until it reaches the "soft ball" stage, at which point the sugar syrup is added to the beaten egg whites. This is easy if one has a standing mixer; those using a hand mixer will have to watch the sugar syrup while simultaneously beating the whites. In either case, when it is time to add the sugar syrup to the whites, **keep it away from the spinning beaters or you will have a web of hardened sugar candy mucking up your mixer.** Instead, let the syrup drizzle down the side of the mixing bowl while you continue to beat the whites. You will be rewarded with stiff shiny peaks of sweet egg whites, which hold the air even after you've folded in the whipped cream, nuts, and other add-ins. If you're entertaining a large group, you can unmold the dessert onto a handsome platter and bring it to the table to serve, perhaps dusting it first with cocoa to disguise the wrinkles left by the plastic wrap. Otherwise, serve your guests individually and keep the remainder in the freezer. This melts quickly.

## Nougat Glacé with Raspberry Sauce

### FOR THE SAUCE

1 bag of frozen raspberries, no sugar, defrosted
1 cup sugar, plus additional to taste
Fresh lemon juice, to taste

## FOR THE ICE CREAM

1 cup sugar

4 large egg whites, at room temperature

1½ cups well-chilled heavy cream

⅓ cup crème de cassis

½ cup unsalted pistachio nuts, lightly toasted in the oven and coarsely chopped

½ cup glacé cherries, coarsely chopped (find these in an Italian grocery)

2 ounces extra-dark fine chocolate, coarsely chopped, or 2 ounces Scharffen Berger cocoa nibs (see Note)

Note: If you're using the cocoa nibs, which can be bitter but add a nice crunch, whirl them briefly with a few pistachio nuts in a food processor just to break them up a bit.

**SERVES 8 (LEFTOVERS CAN BE FROZEN)**

**MAKE THE SAUCE:** In a food processor, purée the raspberries with 1 cup of the sugar and the lemon juice and process the mixture further with additional sugar if desired. Strain the sauce through a fine-mesh sieve into a bowl. Refrigerate.

Line an 11¼ × 4½ × 2½-inch terrine or loaf pan with plastic wrap, leaving a 3-inch overhang on each long side.

**MAKE THE GLACÉ:** In a heavy saucepan, combine the sugar and 6 tablespoons water and cook the mixture over moderate heat, stirring and washing down any sugar crystals clinging to the side with a brush dipped in cold water, until the sugar is dissolved. Boil the mixture over moderately high heat, undisturbed, until a candy thermometer registers 245 degrees F.

While the syrup is boiling, in a large bowl beat the egg whites at medium speed until they hold stiff peaks. With the beaters running, pour the syrup in a slow, steady stream down the side of the bowl into the whites, being careful to keep the syrup from hitting the spinning beaters. Once all of the syrup has been added, continue beating on high speed for 2 to 3 minutes more, until the meringue holds stiff, glossy peaks. Reduce the speed to low and beat the meringue for an additional 8 to 10 minutes, or until it is cooled to room temperature.

In a chilled clean bowl with the electric mixer beat the cream with the crème de cassis until it holds soft peaks. Fold it into the meringue. While folding carefully so as not to lose too much of the air in the meringue, sprinkle in the pistachio nuts, cherries, and chocolate until it is combined well. The cherries tend to be sticky, so be careful that they don't cling to each other in clumps.

Spoon or pour and scrape the ice-cream mixture into the prepared terrine, smoothing the top, and cover it with the overhang. Freeze the mixture for at least 6 hours or overnight. Unmold by folding back the overhang and inverting the terrine onto a serving platter. Remove the plastic wrap.

On each plate, pour $1/4$ cup of the raspberry sauce, and on it place a thick slice of the glacé. Dust lightly with unsweetened cocoa powder or garnish with chopped toasted nuts.

# The Handsome Tutor at Lunch

**Michelle Huneven**

MY OLDER SISTER DID NOT DATE IN HIGH SCHOOL. WE LIVED IN Altadena, California, and both attended John Muir High—a school famous at that time for firing a teacher who refused to shave off a beard (he was later reinstated). This was in the late 1960s, when hair was political, controversial. I had crushes on boys just because they had long hair. My sister's crushes, if she had them, were secret.

She was two years older than I was, and a serious student and violinist. She came home from school, practiced, gave violin lessons to small children, and studied. She emerged from her room to eat dinner, then returned to her lair, shutting the door behind her. After she graduated, she remained at home and enrolled in the local junior college to learn Japanese. Her goal was to move to Japan and study violin and violin pedagogy with Shinichi Suzuki—and eventually she did just that. In the meantime, her college life did not seem so different from her high school years; she left in the morning and returned home around dinner time. After eating with our parents and me, she retired to her room to practice and study. She had a musician's keen ear and was gifted in languages—she was already fluent in Spanish—but Japanese was so much more difficult, she decided she needed a tutor.

"I'm sure you can find one through the college," my mother told her.

My sister decided on another method and confided in me. Being the ever-admiring younger sibling, I was amazed by her strategy. She had determined who was the handsomest Japanese speaker in the college library and, drawing on some untapped reserve of courage, asked him to tutor her.

He agreed.

The handsome tutor, it turned out, was almost thirty years old and himself in need of a tutor. He had been born and raised in Japan and had just moved to California from France, where he'd been for seven years. He spoke Japanese, of course, and was fluent in French, but his English was rudimentary.

As the weeks passed, my parents and I heard a lot about the tutor—how intelligent he was, how handsome, how resourceful. Soon, my sister stopped coming home for dinner. She was eating with him, she said, at a Japanese restaurant across from the school. Then they studied together in the library. She arrived home later and later, proscribed by the last bus, which delivered her around eleven p.m. Her Japanese was improving in leaps and bounds.

In the spring, long after she'd confided in me, my sister told our parents that she and her tutor were officially dating.

Our parents said it was time to meet him. Concerned about the age difference, and the obvious sway he held over their daughter, they were poised to disapprove.

Sensing this, my sister put them off for a month or two—he was studying for a test, she was studying for a test, he'd taken a weekend job escorting Japanese businessmen around Los Angeles. She clearly now wanted to keep him all to herself for as long as she could. But our parents applied a steady pressure. She was eighteen and free, of course, to be with whomever she liked, but so long as she was living under their roof, well, they had a right to know the man she was dating. Now if she were to move out . . .

My sister waited until the right occasion presented itself, when introductions could be made on neutral territory. She announced at dinner one night that the following Saturday, there would be a morning recital of Suzuki-method violin students in West Los Angeles. She needed to be there. If we liked, we could go as a family, she suggested, and the tutor could come with us. She shrugged. Afterward, maybe we could all go out to lunch.

My parents agreed instantly. My mother lost no time in making a reservation at our family's favorite restaurant, Robaire's.

In our family, going to a restaurant was a great luxury. Oh, we ate dinner at a local coffeeshop maybe twice a month, and started out yearly camping trips with diner eggs and hash browns. Otherwise, we ate in a place like Robaire's once or twice a year for a special occasion, a birthday, our parents' anniversary. In all dining venues, we followed a strict protocol: no milk for the kids (there was plenty of milk at home), no cocktails for the adults (you could buy a whole bottle of wine for the price of two glasses), no meat with breakfasts (an entire pound of bacon cost as much as those three meager slices).

Robaire's was a cavernous old candlelit French restaurant on La Brea Boulevard not far from the county art museum. The menu was what I'd now call medium-priced, although back then, the numbers listed discreetly to the right of each item seemed like variously sized guilt bombs, a minefield of extravagance, of instant impoverishment. Each time we went, I would scan the menu and find the one or two priciest items and announce with great, resolute primness, "I will have the Chateaubriand."

"Ho ho ho," my parents would say. "Very funny."

I'd scan the menu again, locate the least expensive items, and choose from among them.

At around twelve years old, I lit on a favorite item, which had two virtues: not only was it inexpensive, it made the waiter stop and look at me with interest. Clearly, not many adolescent girls ordered chicken liver omelets. But I loved the plump envelope of softly cooked yellow egg full of wine-dark sauce and melting braised livers.

When the morning of the recital/introduction arrived, my mother was ill. So my father, my sister, and I set forth without her. I was given no choice but to accompany them, and I was curious enough about my sister's first boyfriend not to resent it.

We drove to a street not far from the junior college, where a slim Japanese man waited for us in front of a modest white apartment building. The tutor was indeed handsome—and

distinctly foreign. He clambered into the back of our Dodge
van next to my sister, then reached forward to shake my
father's hand, then mine.

As my father drove, I stole glances into the back seat. The
tutor's light blue shirt had an oddly cut collar, his beige
pants an unusual nubbly texture, and he carried a shoulder
bag that was so much like a purse, I couldn't stop peering
back at it. I was trying to anticipate my parents' reaction, so
each of his peculiarities was deeply worrisome. In retrospect,
I see that he simply dressed like a European, a Frenchman.
The carrying case. Linen pants.

More strange than anything else was that this slim, good-
looking man was obviously quite fond of my bookish, slightly
overweight sister. Each time I looked in the back seat, they
were clutching and rubbing each other's hands. At the
recital, they nervously kneaded each other's thigh throughout the performance.

Soon enough, we were seated in the familiar, convivial
darkness of Robaire's. My father turned to our guest. "The
food here is excellent. I know, as a student, you don't have
many opportunities to eat in a place like this. So please," he
said. "Have anything you want."

I duly scanned the menu for the most expensive items,
but did not make my usual threat: too shy, I think, on the
unprecedented occasion of meeting the man my sister loved.
A man who, incidentally, ordered a Scotch first thing.
Much to my surprise, my father followed suit.

"Just water," my sister said.

"Water's fine," I echoed.

When the waiter came to take our order, I went first:

chicken liver omelet. My sister, frowning at the menu, needed more time.

The tutor went next. He spoke to the waiter at length in French. I watched his finger stray through the menu; it paused here in the list of appetizers, there in the salads, there again among the entrées. The waiter scribbled diligently. Then the tutor picked up the heavy leather-bound wine list.

I checked my father's face to see how he was taking this. He wore a thin smile, but his eyes were glazed. When his own turn to order came, he said, "The chicken," and snapping the menu shut, handed it to the waiter.

My sister asked for a small dinner salad. "I'm not hungry," she said.

The waiter withdrew. My father, with the same thin smile, turned to the tutor. "So," he said. "Tell me about yourself. Where are you from?"

"Osaka." The tutor answered this and each of my father's subsequent questions with unruffled good cheer. He was in business, a small firm, imports and exports, here to learn English, never married, parents living, and so forth until the first course arrived. *His* first course, that is.

We watched the tutor extricate escargots from their swirled taupe shells and sip white wine. He offered us each a little coil of black meat. My sister gamely opened her mouth.

Next came a pumpkin-orange lobster bisque. Still, he was the only one eating. This appeared not to bother him. He offered my sister a clump of stained white meat. She shook her head. Wine? A sip? What about me?

As intrigued as I was to see items from forbidden areas of the menu materialize at our table, I was far too mortified to sample them. No, no thanks. That's okay, I told him.

Finally everyone's entrées arrived: he'd ordered frog legs, which came battered and were blessedly unrecognizable.

A glum silence reigned. I had never enjoyed my omelet less. My sister's salad was only slightly mussed when removed. My father cleared his plate, swept it clean with a piece of bread.

The tutor's dessert was a thin cross-section of a many-layered gâteau resting in a pool of cream. I could not resist taking a bite, but by then the terror—the sympathetic terror I felt for my sister—made everything taste like wax. Brandy. Coffee. Would his courses ever stop coming?

When the bill arrived, the tutor reached for it, but his was not an aggressive gesture. "No, no, no, I insist," my father said, and while his was not exactly a heartfelt protest, that was that.

On the ride home, my sister and the tutor whispered and giggled in the backseat. My father and I gazed straight ahead. When we reached the tutor's apartment house, my sister surprised us by jumping out as well. "I'll be home after dinner," she said.

Alone with my father, I ventured a comment. "He really seems to like her."

My father's cheek twitched but he said nothing, and we rode the rest of the way home in silence.

My father duly went into a closed-door conference with my mother.

When my sister came home around ten-thirty, my parents presented a unified front to her. They did not approve of the tutor. My sister should stop seeing him immediately. The ensuing fight lasted deep into the night. He was too old, they said. He was inconsiderate. A freeloader, a mooch. At the very least, a big spender of other people's money. Why, his meal alone had cost more than all three of ours together!

Every now and then, my sister's tearful wail soared above the fray. "But you *told* him to order whatever he wanted," she cried. And, "He tried to pay and Dad wouldn't let him!"

All of which is to say that my parents gave my sister no choice in the matter concerning this man. She didn't do it right away, but eventually, inevitably, she married him.

## Robaire's Chicken Liver Omelet

3 large eggs
Salt
Butter
Chicken liver filling (see below)

Beat 3 large eggs and a pinch of salt with a rubber spatula until mixed, no longer. Heat butter in an omelet pan until foamy. Add the eggs. With the spatula, move the cooked eggs and let the uncooked eggs run underneath to the hot surface of the pan. Add the chicken liver filling on one half of the omelet. Fold the omelet over. Cook for a minute. The eggs should be soft.

### CHICKEN LIVER FILLING

5 chicken livers, trimmed of fat and membrane
Flour seasoned to taste with salt and pepper and a few grains of cayenne pepper
2 tablespoons butter
2 tablespoons minced onion
Red wine

Dredge the chicken livers in the seasoned flour and set aside. Heat the butter in a sauté pan until foamy. Sauté the minced onion until wilted over medium-hot heat. Add the chicken livers and brown. Add a splash of wine and enough water to deglaze the pan and make a sauce. Turn down the heat. Cover and cook over low heat until the livers are tender, about 15 minutes. Correct the seasonings. Keep warm while preparing the eggs or make ahead and heat before filling the omelet.

# Yes

## Lan Samantha Chang

SU MEANS "PLAIN," AND TO AN EATER OF CHINESE FOOD IT ALSO means "no meat." *Su jiaozi* are dumplings stuffed with bean threads, chopped shitake mushrooms, cabbage shreds, or greens. *Su ji* is not real chicken but a savory vegetable filling wrapped in tofu skin. The plain cuisine, my *waipuo* claimed, developed out of necessity. To eat su is the province of only the impoverished or the deliberately pure, and su cooking reaches its heights among those who have made a habit of denunciation.

Well into her sixties, Waipuo was a sybarite, a petite but sensuous eater who nursed a long belly under her drab widow's clothes. She loved spicy shrimp served in the shell and all parts of the pig. I remember her sinking healthy teeth into the shining skin of a fat pork joint stewed "red" with soy sauce, sugar, and cloves; or thrusting out her lower lip, indignant at the skimpy dinners served by her daughter, my mother, at our kitchen table in northeastern Wisconsin. She looked with some disdain upon our ordinary lives, comparing our meager family table with the groaning board of a long-ago Shanghai banquet. She took true interest only in the meals she cooked herself and in her best grandchild, my sister Tina, for whom she bought jewelry and knit the prettiest sweaters. Tina and I were close, and I knew she wasn't perfect. I knew she had flirted with several boys and even kissed some of them in the basement; I knew she spent hours daydreaming about boys and that she hid sexy romance novels in her nightstand. But I suspect that even if our grandmother had known about these wanton activities, she would have overlooked them; with her capacity for pleasure she might have understood them.

Waipuo and I had little use for one another. With my height, big bones, and outsize feet, I reminded her perhaps of my studious mother, who had disappointed her by marrying my father. She had nothing against my father personally, but she wanted her daughter with a richer man. A less forgiveable offense lay in my unwillingness to please. While Tina needed only a brief instruction to apprehend or follow Waipuo's lead, I never remembered the old manners she held dear. I dressed sloppily and forgot to comb my hair; I was always reading; I had no semblance of propriety: no *guiju*. I was shapeless, hapless, rudderless. As the third daughter of four, I wallowed in passivity and contempt, in the irresponsible hostility of the powerless. Stubbornly, Waipuo lectured me; she made me curl my hair and taught me how to knit. Sometimes when she looked at me through thick glasses, I had the feeling she wasn't seeing me—rough hair, chapped lips, and sullen gaze—but straining to see something beyond me.

She pretended not to understand English, and I pretended not to speak Chinese; but despite these strategies our interactions were often stormy. "That can't be your complexion. Do you ever wash your face?" "You have no guiju." "You are a mess." At her most incensed, her voice grew dry, and she spat out her lectures with the mechanical percussiveness of an old typewriter. "Without guiju! Without guiju! You must learn guiju!"

One afternoon when I was in my early teens, we came to grief over a sky-blue cabled sweater. Ten long rows back, I had dropped a stitch, and, in my cowardly and avoidant fashion, I failed to acknowledge this when it was discovered. My grandmother unraveled the ten rows, her lower lip swelling with disapproval and disgust. She insisted I replace each row, scrutinizing every stitch and lecturing relentlessly in her dry voice. Finally I exploded. I flung the knitting across the room and ruined it. I shrieked, "Leave me alone!" Another knitting lesson ended.

Later, doing the dishes, I dared to ask my mother if Waipuo had mentioned this quarrel.

"She says you have a temper."

"She was such a pain!"

"She thinks you will become a Buddhist." I heard a hint of curiosity in my mother's voice.

"That's weird!"

I knew Waipuo had recently joined a Buddhist temple in New York. I knew Buddhists did not eat meat, that they took vows of poverty and sought simplicity. But I could not understand what forces would compel my grandmother, or anyone, to move in that direction.

My grandmother was born the spoiled only girl in a family of ten children, to the son of a prominent official serving at the decadent tail end of dynastic rule. This official, my great-great-grandfather, had built a house so grand the grounds required eight dozen streetlights. Such ostentation made the house a target for revolutionaries in 1911. My grandmother survived the fire as an infant, carried out of the house by a maid.

"What happened to the property?" I once asked my mother.

She shrugged. "It's lost."

"Lost? How did they lose it?"

"They spent it all away."

Waipuo was married in 1934, in a hotel wedding in Shanghai. She was four feet, eleven inches tall and weighed ninety-five pounds; when uncoiled her hair, which had never been cut, swept to her knees. She wore a fashionable western wedding dress and a diamond ring. My grandfather took good care of her. In the next few decades, she survived the Japanese invasion, occupation, civil war, and exodus to Taiwan without letting these changes dim the pleasure she found in life. She was a creature entirely at home with her worldly desires. A woman who practiced such financial profligacy that even during the war, when the flesh of any animal was hard to come by, she would squander her husband's money on fresh pork, chicken, and shrimp for one exquisite soup.

My mother was raised by servants, beginning with a wet nurse, and perhaps her serious nature developed as a form of resistance to her own mother's lavishness and interest in fun. She worked hard, first in high school; and then, after my grandfather died, as a scholarship student in the U.S.; and finally, with my father, as a scrimping mother of four. She saved change in an envelope so that her daughters could buy nickel Dilly Bars at Dairy Queen. She counted out the slices of ham to make the lunch meat come out even each week. At night, she rarely left the house and never joined my father in his bridge or mah-jongg games, which reminded her, perhaps, of her childhood evenings spent wishing her mother would stay at home.

"She would play mah-jongg for a week at a time," my mother said. "That's why I hate mah-jongg."

"How did she do that?"

"They would sleep through the day, then get started after a quick dinner and keep going until the sun came up. She loved to gamble."

I imagine Waipuo in those years, a little plump but still beautiful, cackling out her dry laugh and flinging her luck at the bright tiles. Life was catching up to her. The Communist takeover forced her and my grandfather to flee the country. He was ill when they left China and would never again be well; he succumbed to cancer when she was forty-five. After his death, she had no idea how to hold onto his business. The money ran through her fingers and she came to the U.S. to live with her three children, who had crossed the ocean and were living on their wits. My uncles landed on their feet, becoming prosperous businessmen; my mother married an engineer and began her frugal life in northeastern Wisconsin, where she counted pennies and did her own dry cleaning.

When I was twelve, my mother was struck down with a mysterious illness. Although she had always been prone to headaches, stomach trouble, and general frailty, this new malady seized her with a consuming force. She spent days in bed, feverish and exhausted. One by one, her joints and knuckles swelled and grew misshapen. At the age of forty-two, she was diagnosed with rheumatoid arthritis, a chronic and incurable autoimmune disease. She would never again ride a bicycle or weed the garden. She would never walk without pain.

In the face of this unsolvable trouble, my grandmother turned to Buddhism. Her own father had pilgrimaged across the Himalayas, traveling with his ink brushes and six personal servants. Now Waipuo began a more inward journey, alone. My mother's illness sent her in search of answers from a higher power. My father built a prayer table for her room. Waipuo began to spend her mornings on her knees before a little figure of Guan Yin, the goddess of mercy. She passed the evening hours fingering her beads and chanting prayers under her breath. She joined the New York temple on a visit to my uncle. She played the drum during rituals and often stayed at the temple when the monks and nuns went away on pilgrimages and needed a housesitter.

She gave up meat in her early seventies. She did not take to the change with grace. I remember watching her bang around in the kitchen with her lower lip stuck out when she seemed angry at the diet she had chosen. With critical eyes I saw that after she renounced meat she took an even more special interest in food, spending hours in the kitchen, cooking for the family and savoring the smells of our forbidden meals. She made no effort to convert us, but my sister Tina accepted her Buddhism and took a natural interest in learning what it meant. At Dartmouth, Tina majored in anthropology and undertook a research project on eastern religious rituals.

The summer I turned nineteen, Tina arranged to meet our grandmother for a few days at the temple. She planned to attend services and interview the monks and nuns. She would have some time alone with Waipuo, who was getting old. On Saturday, she would meet Hao Ling Fashi, the head of the temple, who had a reputation as a fortuneteller. Then there would be lunch.

"You're coming along on Saturday," my sister said, and I obeyed. It was easier to obey than to learn what I wanted.

On a warm morning in early June, the three of us met in my grandmother's temple on the edge of Chinatown.

The temple smelled strongly of incense and food. The main room was high and square, its walls a pale green tinged with smoke. In its center stood an enormous, garishly appointed statue of the Buddha, looming over an offering table and an enormous urn of incense sticks and ash. That day, the room had been readied for a funeral. A black-and-white photograph of a man hung over the offerings, platters of molded soybean shapes, dumplings, fruit, and paper money.

While our grandmother spoke to Hao Ling Fashi, I followed my sister. We walked to the back wall and gazed at the thousands of flickering red candles there. Followers had purchased each candle in memory of a soul. One of those candles, Tina explained, had been purchased by my grandmother for Huahua, our old dog who had died five years earlier.

"These Buddhists," Tina explained to me, "place the same weight on all souls: the soul of a dog or a human being are the same." This was the principle upon which my grandmother had given up meat.

I envied Tina for her knowledge of these details, but pretended to myself that I did not.

Hao Ling Fashi was a tall, ochre-colored man whose magnificent head rose, with its salt-and-pepper crew cut, from a rough brown robe. He had very large, very square black glasses and his stubbled scalp was spotted with rosacea. As the head of the temple, he was its official fortuneteller. According to my mother, the monks learned divination to detect future donors. This skill had helped the Buddhists survive thousands of years. Waipuo held Hao Ling Fashi in great esteem. She had heard that he was always right; and he wouldn't tell the future of just anyone. People came from far and wide bringing donations to the temple; but sometimes, he would refuse.

Waipuo nudged Tina over to stand before the man. As the older child, she would have her fortune told first.

This took some time and was quite dull. Hao Ling Fashi peered at Tina's hand; then he motioned to Waipuo, and they peered at it together, muttering. Waipuo was always reading our palms; many a knitting lesson had been interrupted thus; but now she looked with guidance, and it seemed to take forever. I was impatient, always, in those days, but Tina's fortune was rendered particularly unendurable by Hao Ling Fashi's choice of a dialect I didn't know. Apparently our fortunes were to be kept secret from us. I shifted on my feet, listening to words slanted, words stunted and changed in tone, familiar words I could not place, unfamiliar words I knew that I would never remember. I felt regretful, and irritated by my regret. I glanced at Tina, whose Chinese was better than mine. Her pretty features worked with concentration, but it was clear that she could not decipher the conversation any more than I.

Then it was my turn. Hao Ling Fashi asked me to stand before him while he examined my palm. He was silent for quite a while, and then he pressed my fingertip until it turned white and watched the color flood back in. He said calmly, in careful English, "You should eat more slowly. Exercise. Eat less grease."

I waited, skeptically. It was a piece of advice I could have found in *Reader's Digest*.

Without further comment, Hao Ling Fashi leaned closer to read my face.

I have no idea what I looked like in those days. Photographs reveal a stranger, often with her eyes shut. I knew I was not a catch, like Tina, who already had a serious boyfriend whom she seemed about to marry. Nor was I unattractive enough to be excused from all appraisal; so I sought to be as nondescript as possible. I did not want to be beautiful if it meant I must be present. Moreover, if I didn't assert myself, didn't care, I would not be forced to acknowledge myself as a creature of such bile. My grandmother was correct. I was a mess, churning with anger and desire and loneliness; a mess of untamed feelings, unacceptable. I wished to be invisible, for invisibility was the closest thing to peace that I could imagine.

Still, I was curious to know what Hao Ling Fashi thought.

Enlarged by the enormous glasses, his calm eyes gave little away. When he spoke, it was with something like surprise.

"*Xiong!*" He spoke the word emphatically. "Xiong," he repeated. I can almost recall him shaking a finger as he spoke. It was a word I knew. It meant, I knew, "fierce." I liked that word in English; it conjured up a vision of tigers and other charismatic predators.

He peered at my palm and tapped it. "*Fa cai,*" he said. So what? I thought. So I would be rich. I had never wanted money.

Then Hao Ling Fashi turned to my grandmother and spoke for several minutes in their rapid-fire dialect.

Later Waipuo told my mother what he had said. But when I questioned my mother, I could only pry from her a few vague pieces of information. She said I would have power and fame, but that my luck would not be steady. I would marry late, she added, frowning. I asked her about Tina, but she wouldn't respond. "She has peach blossom luck," she finally said, but refused to clarify what that meant. I asked every native speaker I knew until I managed to compose a working definition. A person with peach blossom luck is someone too much desired. That's all I was able to discern.

Using a Chinese dictionary, I also learned the connotations of the character *xiong*. "Fierce." "Inauspicious, ominous." A xiong year meant crops would fail, famine would come. A xiong person was terrible, fearful; and as a noun, the word meant an act of violence.

"He never said that," my parents told me, when I asked them about xiong. "He never used that word for you." But I heard him say it. In fact, it pleased me. Whatever Hao Ling

Fashi meant, he did not make light of me. He had seen some-thing in my formless self, something to be reckoned with.

They say the people of the east believe in passivity and fate, and westerners in independence and free will. But I be-lieve it was at the moment of my first contact with Buddhism that I began to see myself as a person who would make her own future, separate from my family, a thing unto myself. I who had lived under Waipuo's skeptical gaze would someday escape this gaze. I would become a woman of force; I would emerge, perhaps darkly, perhaps more fiercely than anyone wanted. The pain of always trying to follow a set of invisible rules would disappear; it would be lost. I would be free.

Leaving the temple, walking with my grandmother and sister, yet newly separate from them, I felt ravenous.

We ate our lunch in a nearby restaurant, wedged into a tiny booth.

It was the last meal I can remember eaten together by the three of us. It was my first meal as a fledgling self. Now I think of this lunch often; it is one of the most vibrant feasts in my memory. In the center of the colorful, odorous restau-rant, my grandmother, sister, and I sit together in a booth. Next to me, Tina takes out her notebook about Buddhism. Tina is twenty-one years old; her smooth brown features are demure and her thick hair falls to the middle of her back. Tina, who will be too much desired. She will be engaged the following year. In six years, she will be divorced, and in two more, remarried.

Across from Tina and me, my grandmother works her chopsticks. She who has been such a creature of the world is now learning to say no to it. With this plain meal she takes one more step along a path she started in her twenties, when she chopped off her own luxurious hair in the interests of modernism. She gave up wearing colors; she gave up China, Hong Kong, and Taiwan. Now she is an old woman living with her children, a vegetarian whose donations to the temple come from the government. In six years she will die of a cerebral hemorrhage, the swift, easy death she prayed for.

While my grandmother and sister chat, I am busy eating. I'm nineteen years old, and I have just said yes to the world. My mind is bright with focus and with unsatisfied hunger. My mutinous passivity shields ambition and desire. Soon I will defy my parents and abandon a more stable job to pursue the life of a novelist. I will move twelve times in fifteen years. I will not marry until the age of thirty-nine, and only then will I begin to recognize how dangerous it is to want things. We never recover from our desires, and must at last wean ourselves away from them, patiently, as my grandmother did.

But I don't know that at this lunch. I am eating, feeding my worldly ambition on the food of monks, the exquisite pure dishes of those who have renounced the world. There are vegetable dumplings in translucent, almost bursting skins, including tiny bits of carrot for the pleasure of their color. Dumplings delicate and savory, each flavor a surprise. There are ribbons of pressed tofu wrapped around savory mushrooms; there are delicious wilted pea leaves of a deep and vibrant green. Everything is simple, everything complex. As I taste these plain dishes more vividly than I have tasted anything before, I understand that there is richness even in plainness, a vividness as marvelous as anything to be found.

# The Place
# We Came From

## Diana Abu-Jaber

NOTHING IS MORE WEIRDLY DISCORDANT THAN WHEN AN ANCIENT world begins to modernize. But Jordan is changing, whether I want it to or not. I first started visiting Jordan in the late 1960s when I was a little girl, each time my immigrant father tried to move us back "home." My family would pack everything up, sell the house, and fly to Amman, and within weeks or months, Dad would become impatient with the slow pace of the city, the crazy drivers, the broken machinery. He'd grown accustomed to the ease and efficiency of life in America. So, inevitably, he would once again give up on his dream of return, and along with my sisters, mother, and me, return in a huff to the States.

Still, even if my father didn't appreciate the dawdling pace or inefficiency of life in Amman, that didn't necessarily mean he wanted it to change. Rhythms are part of the constellation that gives any city its special character. But over the years American-style date books, appointment calendars, and cell phones started to appear in the Middle East. Those were just a few of the changes that I noticed when I returned to my father's country, years later, as an adult. It seemed that shifts had begun at every level of life—including the rituals of eating.

At one time, most meals in Jordan were prepared at home, among families—or, if you had the money, by servants. Socializing was done within homes, and for a little change of pace, young urbanites might all stroll out to the center of one of the traffic circles to the scruffy patches of grass and weeds, some with rickety benches, and hang out smoking cigarettes, watching each other, and talking.

But when I return to Jordan in 1995 for a year of research and writing, many restaurants have appeared: an international plethora of offerings lines the winding, old stone streets of Amman. It's mildly shocking: I wander the streets with a profound sense of disorientation. To my additional surprise, within months of arriving, I find I have a wildly eclectic assortment of friends and acquaintances, expatriates from England, Asia, and Europe as well as all sorts of restless, cosmopolitan Jordanians. Many of these people came (or came back) to Jordan to be with spouses or were transferred to Amman by multinational corporations or diplomatic agencies or schools. The one thing we have in common is that none of us seems to be entirely sure of what we're doing here; even the Jordanian natives speak longingly of traveling to points beyond the horizon—usually meaning the West, America, or the U.K.—toward opportunity or excitement. No one in Jordan seems to have much nostalgia for the old or traditional way of doing things—living with one's extended family, raising a big family, eating at home—and people roll their eyes when I ask about these things.

At the time, I am also writing a novel, I think, but I have little loyalty to it. I live in a state of distraction. I'd thought I was returning to Jordan to discover my family's cultural history, its connection to the dispossessed Palestinians, and its rustic Bedouin origins. But upon arrival, I immediately begin pining for the United States. Every day, I put down my pen when people call, luring me out for drinks, lunches, dinners, or parties. My friends and I go in search of culture and self-indulgence—food, coffee, and talk—walking the long, curvy streets that wend up and down the old hills of Amman. We visit multicolored little Mexican shacks, French bistros with plush tablecloths, and sticky-floored pubs filled with young Jordanians and Irish expats. Frequently the fare is excellent, but the dining-out experience is often mysterious and unpredictable. It's not like dining in, say, Paris or New York, places with a long, polished history of restaurants. But then I discover that, to some, Amman is also a beacon of possibilities and pleasures, as when my friends Jack and Liyanna come for a visit from the West Bank.

Jack and Liyanna are only going to be in Amman for a few nights and I really want to please them. They live in Ramallah, which is beset by curfews, closings, and the general malaise and impoverishment of an occupied land. It's taken us months to arrange this short visit for them, to put together the necessary papers and get them through the checkpoints (they are refused entry to Jordan the first time they attempt to visit and must try again weeks later). After we put away their bags, I ask them where they'd like to eat,

what special food they might be missing. We will cook together, but on their first night in town, I decide to opt for
something different for them, a restaurant. Jack lounges
back in a chair at my empty kitchen table, slides his hands
behind his head, and, in answer to my question, says,
"Ummm . . . French, Italian, Chinese, African, Tibetan,
German, Polish, Mexican, Burmese, Japanese, Peruvian,
Russian, Thai, American, Vietnamese, Spanish . . . did I
leave anything out?"

Liyanna is a little more specific and says she especially
craves biryani rice, so that night, we walk up the street to
Najmi, a place I've heard serves Indian food. I have high
hopes for Najmi, even though I've never visited this place
before; many friends have recommended it. The building itself is unimpressive—long and low, set off by itself on a
small hilltop field surrounded by scrub brush and cement
rubble. One or two incomplete buildings stand nearby, rebar
for dreamed-of but unbuilt second stories sticking out of
their tops.

As we walk up the pitched driveway, I notice someone is
watching us through the restaurant's front window. Before
we can even enter, the host stops us at the door and asks
which cuisine we've come for. We stare at him in silence. "Is
there a choice?" I finally ask.

"The Lebanese or the Italian?" he says impatiently, one
hand curled back on his hip.

"Um . . . I thought you served Indian?" I ask.

He huffs, gives us a scouring up-and-down glare, and for a
moment it looks as if he will not let us in. Unhappily, he ex-
changes his armload of scarlet velvet-bound and betassled
menus for a handful of laminated little brochures. Stiff-

backed, he threads through the table-filled, cavernous, mostly empty formal dining room—where a solitary couple is eating a platter of livid spaghetti and meatballs—to a wooden door, which opens onto a fugue of noise and peppery smoke. "This is where we serve the Indian," he says in a scornful, patronizing way. The back room is crammed with diners, bubbling hookahs, and a brassy, whining Indo-Arab band playing drums and sitars on a tiny platform. Our menus are placed at the center of a table and the offended host stalks away.

To our consternation, the plastic brochures list dishes like chicken in hoisin sauce, shrimp fried rice, and egg rolls. But then we discover the reverse side of the menu is covered with obsessively tiny print describing dozens of dishes from the subcontinent, including columns of curries, biryanis, and tandoori dishes. We order a great deal of food from the waiter, who refuses to write any of it down or even to make eye contact, and then there is a very, very long, suspenseful wait for dinner. While we wait, we talk and listen to the music and drink a soft jasmine tea served in porcelain cups. Occasionally one of us wonders aloud about what the chances are that a menu with such a limitless range could be any good at all. Then another wonders what sort of trauma could have made our waiter such a bitter man.

But when the food arrives, the dishes are a revelation: light and deft, intricate with spices and seductive layers of heat. There are feathery samosas, crackling spicy papadums, perfectly singed chicken kebabs, creamy cucumber raita, elegant, fiery lamb vindaloo, papery-light crepe-like dosai. We eat up everything on the table, mopping every bit of gravy, velvety spinach, and mango chutney with crisp-edged garlic naan. Falling back in our chairs, we need a little time to breathe. Then we are inspired to follow this with an order of hookahs—or *argilehs*, as the Jordanians call them. The waiter carefully stacks the little coals in the argileh's brazier. The coals come in different scents and flavors—of fruits, flowers, and sweets—that pulse lightly but distinctly through the taste of the smoke, intangible yet suggestive as a memory. We draw on the hoses and the candied heat is cooled through the argileh's bubbling water chamber. The chamber makes a satisfying burble as air churns the water and our lungs expand with lush, velvety white smoke, which we exhale in great steams, as if we were breathing fog. It's ineffably satisfying; my head and hands tingle a bit, filled with the humming sensuality of the bubbles, the heat, the scent of it all. It's the Middle Eastern form of brandy and cigars—an exalted state in which to prolong the afterglow of a good meal, to float in a sense of well-being, both in the body and the world.

"This is it, right here," my friend Liyanna says in a silky, blissful way between pulls on her argileh.

"Let's live here," Jack says, exhaling a plume of sweet smoke.

"You mean in Jordan?"

"I mean right here in this restaurant."

We relax as we draw on our argilehs and view the scene. The small dining room is packed with rampaging children, fat babies on shoulders, people who've abandoned their meals at various stages to dance on a platform the size of a dining-room table, hands swirling in modified belly dance through the air. Jack and Liyanna, who both teach at Birzeit University, are either on vacation or fleeing for their sanity—they didn't give many details when they showed up at my door—but

probably it's both. The endlessly jarring disruptions of life in
the West Bank under the Israeli occupation have given Jack a
nervous compulsion to pluck at his hair. His index finger curls
around a single strand at the back of his head before giving a
short, quick tug. Liyanna has whispered that he's starting to
get thin patches all over his scalp. She wants him to go back
to the States to visit some friends and family, eat some good
food, and sleep in a soft bed. But he refuses so adamantly that
she suspects he must be afraid he won't be able to bring himself to return.

Almost nothing is constant in their life. Electricity and
water in their little village is forever fluttering on and off.
The military checkpoints with their high-handed soldiers
have increased in number and bureaucracy so that it can take
hours to drive a few miles. Two days to get a carton of milk.
Jack, an engineer originally from San Antonio, goes around
much of the time in a state just short of pure shocked outrage
and I can see that Liyanna, his Palestinian wife, is generally
preoccupied with the state of Jack's sanity. She touches his
wrist like a worry stone; and no matter where we are or what
we are doing, some part of her gaze seems eternally trained
on him. When she says, "This is it," I know she means not
only the dancing and music and argileh, she also means
happy families, healthy children, dependable electricity,
plentiful food and drinking water. And that her husband—
who has suffered from cruel, bottomless insomnia ever since
they moved to the West Bank ten years ago—has fallen
asleep in his chair despite the bone-rattling racket, one hand
riding innocently on his belly.

Apparently our waiter interprets Jack's slumber as a form
of tribute, because quite unexpectedly he brings us a fine

china bowl filled with what appear to be Swiss butter cookies. But when we ask about meeting the genius polyglot chef who made tonight's feast, he seems mortified, as if we'd asked for a peek at his underwear drawer. "The chef . . . he doesn't like that . . . he doesn't like to leave his kitchen. Ever."

Ah, yes, we murmur, we respect the sensitivity of our genius. "But where is he from?" we pry gently. What could be the starting place for one who roams so freely from nation to nation, speaking the languages of pasta and rice, kebab and stew?

The waiter is clearly the sort who wears his heart upon his sleeve: his interior emotional world shows in his face, and now it's quite clear that he is affronted by our question. "Well, Chef is from Jordan, where else could he be from?" he says.

That's right, we murmur, chastened.

The waiter suddenly decides to have a little heart-to-heart with us. He pulls up a chair and gazes at me and Liyanna with an earnest intensity. "In my opinion," he says, lacing his fingers together in a formal, businesslike manner, "Indian food is . . . fine . . . but it is what I call . . . *low food*. It is what the—" he drops his eyes and indicates the busy room with his veiled gaze, "the *normal people* eat. But here you are—visitors from Russia—it is incredible! You should be eating Chef's masterpieces. Yes, anyone can make the common foods—but he also can prepare the highest of the high."

Which is what? we ask, very curious, and don't bother correcting him about Russia.

Again, the veiled gaze, a mild, humble, modest voice, a nod, as if we won't believe it without some coaxing: "Spaghetti. And meatballs." He gestures toward the window that faces old Amman, where the ruins and columns of the ancient conquerors still mark the center of downtown; where, possibly, King Zeus still floats on his throne, monitoring all feasting. "Roman food," he says.

Jack awakens once Liyanna and I have eaten all the cookies, finished smoking all the coals in the hookah, polished off two pots of sweet mint tea, and are leaning shoulder to shoulder, humming with a tuneless buzz of satisfaction. He presses the inner corners of his eyes, as if the sight of our warm restaurant is a continuation of sleep. He looks at his wife, recognizing her with delight, and she places her hand upon his as if it were a precious piece of jewelry.

"I had the most wonderful dream," Jack says, but then he won't tell us what it was. When we press him, the opinionated waiter, who is clearing our table (still hoping we'll give in and let him serve us some spaghetti) leans in and interrupts our prying. "No, don't do that," he tells me and Liyanna. "Let him keep his dream."

We leave him an immense tip. At the door, he puts us into our coats like a good father and then looks at each of us closely. "You had fine food tonight," he says. I can't tell if he's asking us or confirming this. "When you go back home, I hope you won't forget us." And then, more enigmatically: "You never forget the place you came from."

One of the inescapable realities of dining at restaurants is that it is a business transaction. The lines are clearly drawn. Eating at home is personal in ways even the most intimate restaurants could never be. But even so, a restaurant offers its moment of communion, the shared sacrament of eating together.

Soon, I'll be returning to my home in the States and Jack and Liyanna will try to return to the West Bank. But it will turn out that this night of ease and comfort has broken something open in Jack. Eventually, they will find they have to return to America. Years later, when asked about his time in Ramallah, Jack will say, "It was like a dream."

And the next time I return to Amman, three years later, it will be so developed, I won't recognize it. Car tunnels will run through the old hillsides and towering luxury hotels with a variety of American and European restaurants will have sprung up all over town. The little Najmi Restaurant will be gone, a Starbucks franchise in its place.

But once upon a time, this night existed. It continues to exist as I imagine us, rising from the table, deeply content. The moment of consciousness and life pulses in the black sky over Amman. As we wave to our host and turn out the door, we put our hands to our chests because the wind is picking up, steeper and harder now, washing over the silvery tips of the moon. We walk out into the thin blue night, only very slowly, very gradually, and quietly and gratefully, silent as spirits drifting into the desert.

## The Best and Simplest Yogurt in the World

Blend one cup plain yogurt with one teaspoon lemon juice, one crushed garlic clove, and half a peeled, diced cucumber. Salt if you must. Serve with Indian or Arab food, curry, tagine, roasts, rice. It cools, it refreshes the palate, and it adds a little something.

# Death by Lobster Pad Thai

## A Counter-Phobic Paean to Friendship, Crustaceans, and Oral Transcendence

### Steve Almond

I AM FRIGHTENED OF MANY THINGS: DEATH, MORMONS, STILTON cheese, scorpions, Dick Cheney, the freeways of Los Angeles. But I am perhaps most frightened by lobsters. The spiny antennae, the armor-plated cephalothorax, the serrated claws—they are, to my way of thinking, giant, aquatic cockroaches that can snap your finger off.

I mention this because for the past few years now I have been heading up to Maine to visit my pals Tom and Scott, and specifically to partake of the transcendent Lobster Pad Thai that they prepare together, lovingly, painstakingly, over the course of a long, drunken summer afternoon.

And because, this past summer, I played an unwitting (and unwilling) role in the preparation of the greatest single Lobster Pad Thai in the history of man. And of lobster.

It began with a simple request: would I be willing to stop by an establishment called Taylor Seafood to pick up some things?

Of course I would.

"We'll need a pound or two of shrimp," Tom said. "And some lobsters."

I swallowed.

"They're selling four-pound lobsters at a great price."

I now spent perhaps half a minute trying, and failing, to imagine myself picking up a four-pound lobster, with my actual hands.

"Hello?" Tom said. "Hello?"

"Yes," I said miserably.

"Did you get that?"

"Yeah. I got it. Four-pound lobsters."

"Four of them. We'll reimburse you when you get here."

*You'll reimburse me*, I thought, *if I live that long.*

I'm not sure how many of you out there have seen a four-pound lobster. (Most of what you see in the grocery stores or restaurants are less than half that.) Neither my girlfriend, Erin, nor I was quite prepared.

The creatures were—as Tom would later observe, unhelpfully—larger than many newborn infants. Their tails were Japanese fans. Their claws were baseball mitts. They squirmed unhappily as the guy working the counter packed them into flimsy plastic bags. The biggest one swung toward me before he was lowered down and I am here to tell you there was murder in those beady, stalked eyes.

Yes, of course the claws were bound with thick bands. The animals had been rendered sluggish by ice and air. They were in no condition to attack. And yet . . .

And yet the true phobia is marked not by the threat of actual harm, but by a fantasy in which the subject imagines harm into being. Thus, as Erin drove north, as the bags rustled about in the backseat, I felt certain the lobsters were merely *pretending* to be sluggish and out of sorts while, in fact, communicating with one another via their antennae, biding their time, preparing to launch a coordinated attack. How might this happen? I didn't know exactly. I envisioned them using their tails in a sort of ninja-pogo maneuver, bouncing from dashboard to emergency brake, while snapping at our fragile extremities.

Thus I kept close watch over the bags until such a time as we arrived at the home of Scott and his partner Liza, who is Tom's sister. Also on hand for our arrival were Tom's lovely wife, Karen, and their two darling children, Annabel (age: *almost* eight) and Jacob (age: four), all of whom gathered in the kitchen as we lugged the four heavy bags inside.

Scott immediately opened a bag and hoisted one of our purchases out. He whistled admiringly while Jacob, perhaps the only other one of us who realized the danger we were in, took a step backward.

Some background is in order.

Fifteen years ago I flew down to Miami to interview for a job at the alternative weekly and, after two days of vapid schmoozing, decided not to take the job. Then two things happened: I ate my first bowl of black bean soup. And I met Tom, the managing editor, for a cup of coffee. I felt, almost immediately, that I had found a long-lost older brother, the kind of guy who might rescue me from my own glib excesses, both as a writer and as a human being.

There is plenty to explain this. We're both Jews, suburban depressives, painfully susceptible to the song of language. In the four years we spent together in Miami, Tom taught me most of what I know about writing. He also taught me how to eat.

I can remember practically every meal I've eaten with him over the years: not just the epic, five-course Am Ex–buster partaken at Kennebunkport's hallowed White Barn Inn, but the pillowy gnocchi in vodka sauce ordered from a tiny Miami trattoria called Oggi, as well as any number of grilled fryers, exquisitely prepared by Tom himself, using butter, rosemary, and sea salt.

The man has always been something of a foodnik. But in recent years, his culinary interests have bloomed. Part of this is due to Karen, whose abilities are of such a caliber that she routinely enters (and wins) national recipe contests. But it is Scott, his cheery brother-in-law, who has been his most concerted enabler.

Karen and Tom are deeply in love, and cooking has become the purest expression of their mutual devotion. For a number of years, they prepared crab cakes together. A few years ago, they decided to undertake lobster pad thai.

Tom's reasoning was based on the following factors:

1. He refuses, on principle, to eat lobster outside the state of Maine;

2. His central goal, therefore, when visiting Scott and Liza each summer is to eat lobster every single day;

3. The rest of his family, especially his children, do not care to eat lobster every single day;

4. The pad thai format is one way of sneaking lobster past these ungrateful philistines;

5. The recipe plays to Scott's strengths as a cook: an ability to organize and prep tremendous amounts of ingredients (what the French call, somewhat grandly, *mise en place*).

It is Liza's contention that her brother Tom employs one additional factor, namely that this recipe calls for the use of every single utensil in her kitchen.

To return to the scene of my terror: Scott was holding one of the lobsters in his hand, sort of waving it about, so that its claws clacked like castanets. Jacob and I were not amused. Eventually, the lobsters were shuttled down to the basement fridge. The people rejoiced. (At least, I rejoiced.) Erin and I were fed many scones. A miniature golf excursion was proposed, then a long discussion concerning Liza's latest sandwich creation, a lobster roll Reuben, which sounded obscene, delicious, and capable of clogging a major coronary artery at fifty paces.

An hour or so after noon, Tom and Scott stood up and looked at one another and announced (in the same way I

imagine the lead climbers announce an assault on the sum-
mit of Everest) that it was *time to get started*.

I feared this would mean a reappearance of the lobsters,
but there was a good deal to be done before that. The chefs
use a recipe from Jasper White's noble volume, *Lobster at
Home*, one White attributes to Gerald Clare. As with most
Asian recipes, it calls for various esoteric ingredients
(shrimp paste, fish sauce, Thai basil, cilantro), all of which
must be precisely measured, poured, mixed, whipped, and
variously sliced.

It may well be true that Tom and Scott use every single
utensil in Liza's kitchen. But it is equally true that they have
a fantastic time doing so.

Indeed, for me, the second great pleasure of the Lobster
Pad Thai ritual (after the eating, at which we will arrive in
due time) is watching these two commandeer the kitchen.
Their style, in terms of grace and economy of motion, calls
to mind Astaire and Rogers, though in terms of alcoholic
consumption Martin and Lewis might be closer to the mark.

Scott does most of the blade work and it says something
profound about both his skills with his trusty eight-inch
Wüsthof Classic, and my own culinary incompetence, that I
have watched the man julienne lemongrass for a full ten
minutes.

Both chefs do a good bit of punning, with Tom—a long-
time headline writer—taking the lead. (To give you a flavor
of his style, consider this groaner, which topped the review
of a particularly abject Chinese eatery: WONTON NEGLECT.)

These shenanigans compose a kind of theater in the
round, given that the kitchen is the home's central hub, and
given that their pace is, to put it charitably, a leisurely one.

It is not uncommon to hear Liza and/or Karen observe that they could make the same meal in an hour, rather than six. Scott and Tom are entirely impervious to such kibitzing.

This is what I find so enchanting: that two men should lose themselves in the spell of collaboration. My own experience, growing up with two brothers, did not include group cooking. We preferred a regimen of beating one another to a pulp.

So Scott and Tom were having a swell time cooking, and I was having a swell time watching them and Liza and Karen were having a swell time both not having to cook and gently mocking their husbands for being slowpokes; the kids were climbing all over Erin. The afternoon was cooling off. The ginger had been minced, the scallions finely chopped.

"Is it time?" Tom said.

Scott nodded and went out back to fire up the propane-heated Turkey Fryer that he and had Liza bought a few years earlier (I believe I've conveyed that they're foodies). This could mean only one thing: the reappearance of the lobsters.

Yes, up they came from the basement. Scott carried two of them outside and lowered them, tail first, into the scalding water. Erin, who is a vegetarian on moral grounds but eats seafood, wanted no part of this. None of the females did, actually. Scott and Tom were interested in a purely scientific sense: How many four-pound lobsters could fit in your standard Turkey Fryer? (Answer: two, and just barely.)

In the end, Jacob and I were left to watch the pot and its unhappy crustaceans. I am sorry to report that they did not die immediately. One in particular did a good bit of writhing before giving up the ghost.

"Is it still alive?" Jacob said.

"No," I said. "Those are just death throes."

"But it's *moving*."

"Yes, that's right. But sometimes an animal makes little movements after it has already died."

Jacob looked at me skeptically.

"Well, what's that stuff?" he asked finally.

The lobsters were emitting strings of pearly, coagulating liquid.

"That's . . . that's . . . I don't know exactly."

Jacob had been curious about the lobster boiling in the way of morbid four-year-olds, but this latest development exceeded his tolerance. He headed back inside.

The lobsters were dead now, no question. Their shells were turning a luminous red beneath a veil of briny steam. I had watched them perish. I felt bad about this. They were innocent creatures, after all. Terrifically ugly and potentially lethal, but only if I found myself on the ocean floor, a place I did not often find myself.

Tom and Scott appeared. Their central concern was timing. How long did it take to parboil a four-pounder? Scott poked at one of the lobsters. I decided that I probably needed a beer.

In terms of lobster guilt, the cooking phase was only a prelude. For the central scene of the entire pad thai drama resided in the gathering of the partially cooked lobster meat, which required the complete destruction of each animal's exoskeleton, and the scrupulous removal of every single morsel therefrom.

To bolster this effort, Tom had bestowed upon Scott several Christmases earlier an implement which has since come to be known (to them, at least) as *The Eviscerator,* a pair of truly fearsome kitchen shears used to cut through the shell of a lobster. Also used was the traditional claw hammer. The other members of the family gave the kitchen a wide berth.

I'm not sure that I can describe the action adequately, other than to say that it made open-heart surgery look relatively tame. This was nothing like the dainty dissections performed by casual diners on restaurant lobsters. It was carnage, an orgy of twisting and snapping and hacking and smashing and poking and the emission of numerous fluids.

To say that Scott and Tom enjoyed this ritual is to understate the case. They conducted their business in a giggling ecstasy. This was a treasure hunt, with gratifying elements of gross-out humor.

Tom peeled off the top of one tail to reveal a dark, veiny line.

"What's that?" I said.

"Back end of the digestive system," Scott said.

"It's full of shit," Tom said.

"The shitter," Scott said.

"The poop pipe," Tom said.

They had each drunk about a six-pack.

There was also a great deal of green gunk, which is called tomalley [insert your own pun here] and is technically, somehow, the lobster's liver. Scott would later inform me, rather against my will, that he and Tom sometimes smear tomalley on a piece of bread, a snack he describes as "pungently tasty." (On a related though unnecessary health note, Scott felt compelled to warn me that tomalley should not be consumed by pregnant women or children, because it

contains toxins, which he claims, implausibly, can be coun-
teracted by the consumption of beer.)

The harvest went on for nearly an hour, because the four-
pounders were so incredibly large and because both men pride
themselves on a thorough evacuation of all body cavities.

It is a strange thing to see the source of your phobia sys-
tematically disemboweled. It made me feel guilty again.
These lobsters were senior citizens, after all. They might
have been grandparents. For all I knew they had been involved in the labor movement. I saw them scuttling feebly
along the ocean floor, muttering curses at the agile, young
lobsters, lining up for the early-bird specials on krill.

It was time for me to go into the living room.

When I returned a half hour later, a large silver bowl sat
on the counter, brimming with glistening lobster meat. It
was more lobster than any of us had ever seen. We took
turns lifting the bowl and trying to guess how much was in
there.

The formal weigh-in: 5.7 pounds.

Dusk was now approaching. The shadows on the back lawn
had grown long. Tom and Scott took some time to clean up
the kitchen, then devoted themselves to the preparation of
a batch of Vietnamese spring rolls, which were to be served
in honor of Annabel's upcoming birthday, along with *nuoc
cham*, a tasty lime-juice-and-fish-sauce dip, which the birthday girl (somewhat predictably, according to Tom) refused
to eat.

This was, in its own way, an involved process, one that required wrapping noodles, shrimp, vegetables, and cilantro in
fragile rice paper. I was even more impressed by the notion

that an almost-eight-year-old child would request such a delicacy. My own ideal meal at that age consisted of Chef Boyardee Beefaroni, Ho Hos, and Orange Crush.

With the spring rolls done, Tom and Scott turned to the main event: stir-frying. Owing to the sheer volume of the batch, this had to be done in two shifts. Scott made sure the right ingredients were going into the wok at the right intervals and Tom stirred, somewhat frantically. First peanut oil and the lobster (the smell was dizzying), then ginger, lemongrass, chili paste, shrimp paste, sugar, rice stick noodles, fish sauce, lemon and lime juice, scallions, and egg.

The formal recipe calls for this stew to be dished up in separate bowls, with peanuts, bean sprouts, and cilantro. Then, and I quote, "Garnish with lime wedge and sprigs of Thai basil and *crisscross the lobster antennae over the top.*" (Italics mine.)

Thankfully, Tom and Scott dispensed with the froufrou approach and simply made up two huge, communal bowls. We gathered on the screened-in porch. For a few moments, we could only stare at the lobster pad thai. It was like the gastroporn on the Food Network: too beautiful for our mouths.

Then someone (I suspect me) spooned a portion onto my plate and all hell broke loose.

I must note here that I am generally not a fan of pad thai. Because often, in restaurants, the pad thai has been sitting around for a while and it gets dried out and—owing to some strange alchemy of, I think, the rice noodles and the fish sauce—smells like old socks.

This pad thai, however, was so fresh, so exquisitely prepared, as to explode on the tongue: the aromatic herbs, the loamy snap of the bean sprouts, the citrus juices, the chewy noodles, the crunchy peanuts and, at the center of the action, the sweet succulence of the lobster. I can't begin to describe the experience of this pad thai; words are inadequate, because all of these flavors and textures were being experienced simultaneously, actually interacting in the course of each bite.

And here's what made the whole thing so special: Tom and Scott were right in front of us, downing impressive quantities of wine and beaming. They had cooked this feast for us, for our enjoyment, and just as much for themselves, for the sheer pleasure of a thing created together.

It made me think of all the stories Tom and I had worked on over the years—more than a hundred. It was what Tom thrived on, the chance to guide a process, to help headstrong schmucks like me get my sentences in order, to usher beauty into the world.

And I thought of all the Monday nights we drove out to the Miami Shores Bridge Club for three hours of cutthroat duplicate under the yellow lights, how deftly Tom played, and how patient he was in the face of my incessant over-bidding.

It made me a little choked up, to think of all the history between us and how we could never have that back.

People were offering toasts now. To the intrepid chefs. To the lobsters. To The Eviscerator. We had been at the table for nearly two hours. The candles were burning down. The kids had gone to bed. I was on my fourth serving.

There was some debate over whether this was the best pad thai Tom and Scott had ever prepared. I did not see how one could make a better pad thai, and I said so. Then, after checking with the proper authorities, I began to eat directly out of the giant bowl.

The rest of the evening begins to get a little blurry. I believe I suggested that Tom and Scott consider opening a restaurant dedicated exclusively to lobster pad thai (suggested name: *Booth & Claw*), though there is some chance that I merely thought this to myself.

I know there was a dessert and that it involved chocolate. We eventually went inside and played a rather silly game of something or other. For the most part, we sat in stunned gratitude, digesting.

The next morning, Erin and I had to return to Boston. We did so reluctantly, and only after securing a large plastic container stuffed with pad thai. It was half-gone before we left Maine.

# About the Contributors

DIANA ABU-JABER'S newest book is a food memoir entitled *The Language of Baklava*. She has also published two novels, *Crescent* and *Arabian Jazz*. She teaches at Portland State University in Portland, Oregon, and lives part-time in Miami.

STEVE ALMOND is the author of two short-story collections, *My Life in Heavy Metal* and *The Evil B.B. Chow and Other Stories*, and the nonfiction book *Candyfreak: A Journey Through the Chocolate Underbelly of America*. His new book, a novel cowritten with Julianna Baggott, is called *Which Brings Me to You*. He lives in Somerville, Massachusetts, and needs to go on a diet.

AIMEE BENDER is the author of three books, most recently the short-story collection *Willful Creatures*. Her fiction has been published in *GQ*, *Granta*, *Harper's*, *Tin House*, *McSweeney's*, and elsewhere, as well as heard on PRI's *This American Life*. She lives in Los Angeles, teaches at the University of Southern California, and is very fond of food.

AMY BLOOM is a practicing psychotherapist and the author of two short-story collections, two novels, and a book of essays. She teaches at Yale University in New Haven, Connecticut, and cooks.

IAN SAMANTHA CHANG was born and raised in Appleton, Wisconsin. She is the author of a short-story collection, *Hunger*, and a novel, *Inheritance*. She lives in Iowa City, Iowa, and teaches at the University of Iowa Writers' Workshop.

HENRI COLE is the author of five collections of poetry, most recently *Middle Earth*, which was a finalist for the Pulitzer Prize.

ANDRE DUBUS III is the author of *The Cage Keeper and Other Stories*, and the novels *Bluesman* and *House of Sand and Fog*. He lives in Massachusetts with his wife and three children.

MICHAEL GORRA is the Mary Augusta Jordan Professor of English at Smith College, where he has taught since 1985. His books include *After Empire: Scott, Naipaul, Rushdie* and *The Bells in Their Silence: Travels Through Germany*. He cooks for his wife and daughter in Northampton, Massachusetts.

MICHELLE HUNEVEN is the author of two novels, *Jamesland* and *Round Rock*. She was a restaurant critic and food writer in Los Angeles for most of two decades. Now she is an avid organic gardener and home cook in Altadena, California.

DAVID LEHMAN has written six books of poetry, most recently *When a Woman Loves a Man*. His prose books include *Signs of the*

*Times: Deconstruction and the Fall of Paul De Man*. He initiated *The Best American Poetry* in 1988 and continues as series editor of the annual anthology. He teaches in the graduate writing program at the New School for Social Research in New York City, and has edited *The Oxford Book of American Poetry*.

MARGOT LIVESEY was born and grew up on the edge of the Scottish Highlands. After taking a B.A. in literature and philosophy at the University of York in England, she spent most of her twenties in Toronto, writing and working in restaurants. Subsequently she moved to America where she has taught in various colleges and universities, including Williams College and the University of Iowa Writers' Workshop. She is the author of five novels, including *Eva Moves the Furniture* and, most recently, *Banishing Verona*. She lives mostly in Boston and is writer-in-residence at Emerson College.

PETER MAYLE is the author of several books, including *A Year in Provence*, and he lives in Provence. His hobbies include reading, writing, and lunch.

ELIZABETH MCCRACKEN is the author of two novels and a collection of short stories. She still won't touch Marmite, even for love.

CLAIRE MESSUD is the author of four books, most recently the novel *The Emperor's Children*. She lives in Somerville, Massachusetts.

SUE MILLER has written seven novels, a collection of short stories, and a memoir about her father and his death from Alzheimer's disease.

ANN PACKER is the author of *Mendocino and Other Stories* and *The Dive from Clausen's Pier*. She lives near San Francisco.

RICHARD RUSSO is the author of five novels, including the Pulitzer Prize–winning *Empire Falls*, as well as a collection of short stories and numerous screenplays and essays. He lives in Maine.

JANE STERN has written more than thirty books with her husband, Michael Stern, many of which have been about American food. As a couple, they are best known for their book and website called *Roadfood*. Stern is also a volunteer emergency medical technician. The movie *Ambulance Girl*, starring and directed by Kathy Bates, was based on Stern's book of the same name, in which she wrote about her work in the field of emergency medicine.

MICHAEL STERN is the coauthor, with his wife, Jane, of more than thirty books about popular culture and American food and they currently write a monthly column called "Roadfood" in *Gourmet* magazine. It was in the early 1970s, while working on a degree in film history at Columbia University, that he set in motion the events that led to his most heinously memorable meal.

MICHELLE WILDGEN is a senior editor at *Tin House*. Her novel, *You're Not You*, was published in 2006 by Thomas Dunne/St. Martin's Press. Her work has appeared in *Best New American Voices 2004*, *Best Food Writing 2004*, and elsewhere.

# Also edited by Douglas Bauer

## Prime Times
*America's favorite writers take on America's favorite pastime: watching TV.*

Everybody loves TV. Even writers, those high-minded intellectuals, secretly succumb to the pleasures of television. In twenty-three essays ranging from humorous to moving, today's best writers delve into the world of sitcoms, dramas, and infomercials. From Nick Hornby on his love of *The West Wing* to Henry Louis Gates, Jr., on *Amos 'n' Andy* and civil rights programs on television, the essays collected in *Prime Times* give us an intimate view of their authors and the impact television has had on their lives.

Prime Times
1-4000-8114-9
$12.95 paper ($19.95 CAN)

Available from Three Rivers Press
wherever books are sold.